How to Publish
Your Own
Magazine

Written and Illustrated by
DON RICE

David McKay Company, Inc.
New York

To Aaron
who enjoys publishing his own magazine

Becoming a Publisher

Designing the Magazine

Finding Readers

☐ **Bill me***
☐ **Bill my compan**
☐ **Check enclosed**

*Your subscription will comm
with first available issue
after receipt of payment

Miscellany

BECOMING A PUBLISHER

The very first cover of TIME*

In 1923, Henry R. Luce and his friend Briton Hadden borrowed $10,000 and founded *Time*. This printing empire grew to include, among other things, *Fortune, Life, Sports Illustrated,* Time-Life Books, and even television productions. Chances are, you do not have $10,000. But no matter. If you have $25 or $25,000 there are certain principles that you must know before founding *your* publishing empire.

We are going to assume that you have extremely limited financial resources and that you must perform most of the magazine's operations yourself (but for the actual printing). Even if you can afford to have all the many operations done for you, you should be familiar with every step along the way. You will want to know these, not only so that you will be aware of the physical limitations that are to be imposed on you, but also so that you can take advantage of the great possibilities that will open up. And, too, you should be able to supervise the entire operation from beginning to end. You can't do that unless you know what you are talking about.

Reading this book will not make you an expert publisher, an expert editor, or an expert anything else. But you will learn enough, if you follow these directions, to publish a magazine—at least one issue. As a guide, we will be going through the step-by-step process of publishing a little magazine (the general term for non-commercial periodicals.)

How successful you will become with your little mag depends on your ability to write, edit, organize, prepare, and distribute the finished product. Your level of commitment to the project will also determine your success or failure. If your basic idea is no good, then no amount of commitment or expertise can save it. Conversely, a good idea poorly executed cannot succeed.

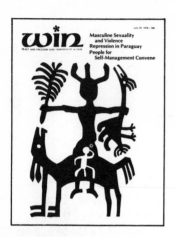

What Kind of Magazine

Presumably, you already have some idea of the sort of magazine it is that you wish to publish. Most little mags fall in one of the following categories: literary, special interest, and political.

Literary mags publish poetry, short stories, essays, parts of novels, satires, plays, and, quite often, drawings and photographs.

Special interest mags can be "fanzines" (fan magazines on such topics as science fiction or rock music), essays on just one particular author's life and works, archaeology, backpacking, films—you name it.

Political mags range from Nazi to Women's Lib, from Gay Power to Black Power, from Alternative Lifestyles to Republicanism. There's a little mag being published somewhere in the United States for probably any variety of political thought that you can imagine.

Easily the most popular form that little mags take is that of the literary review. Under this very general category an editor has much more freedom to select from a wide assortment of articles and artwork; one

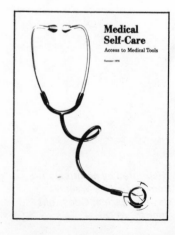

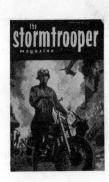

isn't restricted to just articles of interest to railroad engineers, for example.

As editor of a literary journal you can publish almost anything, though it may develop that your readers will come to expect certain standards, a continuity from one issue to the next, whether it be the inclusion of many line drawings or no line drawings; no poetry that rhymes or all rhyming poetry; experimental prose or very traditional prose.

You should make some decisions along these lines right at the start, but be willing to modify them should you discover that you might be more able to please your readers (and yourself) by altering your editorial slant in one way or another.

Why Do They Do It?

In past editions of the *Directory of Small Magazine/Press Editors and Publishers*, the individuals listed were given the opportunity to give their reasons for editing and publishing a little mag. Here are some of the responses:

"Nobody will let me edit a big magazine."—**Bill Zavatasky, SUN**

"I edit because I enjoy it & I try not to rationalize myself into any more of a reason.."—**Larry Robert Zirlin, SOME**

"I'm insane."—**George Wood, THE ABOVE GROUND REVIEW**

"For pleasure and to provide an opportunity for authors and readers to get together outside of the preempted field of the mass culture communications media."—**John Westburg, NORTH AMERICAN MENTOR MAGAZINE**

"The sheer joy of it!"—**Gordon Weaver, MISSISSIPPI REVIEW**

"Ego trip."—**William Wantling, PENTABARF**

"To help others do the same—to encourage as many people as possible to express themselves in print."—**Mitch Waldo, AMERIKAN PRESS SYNDICATE**

"It appeals to my ego or vanity but not to my pocket book other than to deplete the latter."—**Merlin Teed, MERLIN'S MAGIC**

"We all have our idiosyn-crasies."—**Richard Tagett, MAN-ROOT**

"When you find out why, please be sure to let me know! But, I do love poetry and poets."—**A. M. Sterk, POETRY ILLUSTRATED**

"To inform and entertain readers. To accomplish some creative goals. To make a difference." —**James Spada, THE EDWARD M. KENNEDY QUARTERLY**

"To give an opportunity to talented experimental writers to be published."—**George Drury Smith, BEYOND BAROQUE**

"For fame and glory. Also, I suspect, a touch of premature senility. What did you expect me to say?"—**Karen Rockow, UNICORN**

"To encourage literature in my region and state."—**William Reich, LOCK HAVEN CHAPBOOK SERIES**

"Being in contact with creative persons and their words—I like it immensely."—**Rosemary Polzin, CLOVEN HOOF**

"As a teacher, helps serve my function to educate in a specialized area of interest." —**Dario Politella, SYLLABUS**

"To try to counteract the tendency to careless and trivial work being hawked around as literature and philosophy; work which has no genuine basis in living, growing minds."—**Walter Perrie, CHAP-MAN**

"Established presses are largely closed to new writers and new perspectives. They depend on a 'star system' and on the fashionable Zeitgeists."—**OPEN CELL COMMUNE**

"For the fine madness of it."—**Allen Neff, KARAMU**

"Egotism."—**Arthur Moyse, ZERO ONE**

"I'm a masochist."—**Idell, MATRIX**

"There is always room for another good one."—**David Holliday, SCRIP**

"Out of curiousity: to see how well (badly) I do. Also out of a sense of achievement—on my own standards; not from any praise I may get."—**John Harvey, BALTHUS**

"After the usual ego thing, the magazine keeps me around things going on without burning me out."—**James Haining, SALT LICK**

"To keep my sanity; so I'll be reminded that there are people out there trying also."—**Neil Greenberg, FRAGMENTS**

"Because establishment publishing is now too concerned with profit-motive & small magazines are able to publish work for its intrinsic value alone. Having always been associated with publishing & bookselling, I value my editorial freedom on a small magazine."—**Janet Gordon, ANTHOLOGY**

"It's akin to drinking."—**Peter Finch, SECOND AEON**

"Because the need to do so is there and because no one else would print my poetry!"—**Brian Felder, THE BUMMER**

"I'm a sucker for punishment!"—**Gerald England, HALLAMSHIRE & OSGOLDCROSS POETRY EXPRESS**

"Because I have nothing else to do with my time."—**Roger Edwards, OUTSIDER**

"Vanity, vanity, all is vanity. And besides, I enjoy the sense of unlimited power."—**Don Dorrance, ERRATICA**

"I edit a little mag either because I'm hopelessly insane, or else because I'm fighting to stay sane—I hope it's the latter." —**Robert Currie, SALT**

"The small mag is one of the few practical answers to scholarly bull."—**Robert J. Conley, THE BLACKBIRD CIRCLE**

"It gives me a chance to have an identity separate from my work or marriage: something of my own."—**Jane Card, HYACINTHS AND BISCUITS**

"Because I can't stop it."—**Paul Blake, THE SNAIL MAGAZINE**

"It is a life-time habit I have not been able to break,"—**Maurice Beebe, JOURNAL OF MODERN LITERATURE**

"Inescapable compulsion. Fun. Opportunity to make an honest living. Because I'm better at it than at writing poems. None of the above."—**Alan Austin, BLACK BOX**

"There is no way to answer this well or conclusively. If anyone really wishes to know, they may come visit; I'll spend some time with them."—**Tom Ahern, DIANA'S MONTHLY**

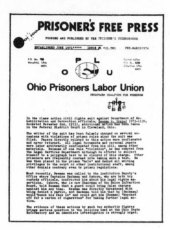

Selecting What to Publish

There are many arrangements that you can make for setting up the "machinery" by which you are going to choose those pieces that you will publish. If you are the sole proprietor there is no problem: publish whatever you please.

It could be, though, that you have one or more partners in this venture. Decide before the very first issue just how selections are going to be made. There are little mags who have an editorial board with every member having an equal say—and nothing gets published without unanimous consent. Some editorial boards divide the selection process among the members and each is alloted a certain number of pages to fill in each issue: a fiction editor, a poetry editor, a

photo editor, etc. There are still others who have a rotating editorship. One person is responsible for the contents of the first issue, another for the second, and this sequence runs its course before starting anew. through all the editors.

To avoid a lot of squabbling (and it's amazing how much bad feeling can be generated among otherwise good friends over what's to be published) settle the matter before you start.

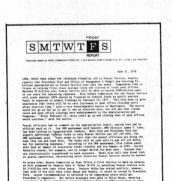

Finding Material to Publish

NO MATTER WHAT YOUR FRIENDS PROMISE YOU, DO NOT DEPEND ON THEM TO PROVIDE YOU WITH ENOUGH MATERIAL TO PUBLISH YOUR MAGAZINE!

Everybody has a great idea for an article, a short story, a poem, something. But just try and get it before the deadline. There are more excuses than you can imagine for not submitting a short story when it is due, but you will hear them all if you depend on your friends.

The problem is this: *Writing is hard work*. It's one thing to come up with a great plot for a short story—that's easy enough. But actually to sit down at the typewriter and commit it to paper is something else. Not only that—and this will hurt—your friends don't really take this magazine project of yours seriously. They'll promise faithfully to deliver, but when it comes right down to it, they think that watching television or going skiing or doing *anything* else is more important than meeting that deadline.

There's yet another problem with friends: Can they really write well? What happens when you, in your editorial capacity, decide to change something they've written? They get insulted, that's what. Who are you, they'll want to know, to presume to change even one immortal comma? To avoid a fight, or to avoid hurting your friend's feelings, you end up publishing a piece of trash—and then you're embarrassed by it. Unless your friends are more understanding, reasonable, talented and reliable than most people, you'd best forget about them as contributors to your magazine on any regular basis. Rely on them if you want, but remember: You were warned.

If not your friends, then who? Listen, there are thousands of people out there who *can* write and who, in fact, have already written their articles and short stories and poetry, and who *yearn* to have their material published in your magazine even though it doesn't yet exist. Use them.

How do you find them? It's easy enough. Make sure that your magazine is listed in the *International Director of Little Magazines and Small Presses.* [See Appendix] Once listed there, the mailman will make regular stops at your house with armloads of manuscripts. If you're planning on publishing before the next issue of the *Directory* appears (it's published annually) you can advertise your needs free. There are a number of little mags, newsletters, and directories that will be happy to carry the announcement that you are planning to publish a magazine and that you are looking for certain types of material. [See Appendix] Do this and you will probably find that you have more material submitted than you can use. Many publishers try to have enough material on hand to fill two or three future issues.

What do you have to pay for the material? Nothing. Nothing, that is, except for two or three (or even one, if you want) copies of the issue in which the material appears. You will not be cheating them. All of the writers will have different motives for wanting to be published, but virtually none of them will expect to be paid. Just getting into print is all they ask.

It's a nice idea to print, somewhere in the magazine, some *Notes on Contributors*. After you have selected articles and stories, you should write to the authors telling them you have done so, and asking them to provide you with *short* paragraphs about themselves. (The paragraphs probably won't be short, but you can edit them.)

It might be that you want to use a particular article, but feel that something in it should be changed.

Thank you for sending us your manuscript. It has been read by one or more of our editors. The return of your work does not necessarily imply criticism of its merit, but may simply mean that it does not meet our present editorial needs. We regret that circumstances do not allow individual comment.

THE EDITORS

FICTION INTERNATIONAL
DEPARTMENT OF ENGLISH
ST. LAWRENCE UNIVERSITY
CANTON, NEW YORK 13617

Dear Contributor:

Thanks for sending the enclosed material for our consideration. After careful study we have decided that it does not fit our present needs.

We do appreciate your thinking of us and hope for your continued interest in our magazine.

Cordially,

THE EDITORS

Since you're not paying anything, you have the obligation to tell the writer just what it is you're changing and ask for his or her permission to do so. You will almost certainly be granted permission if your suggested change is reasonable. If the author doesn't want it changed, well, then it's up to you whether or not you use the piece.

Many of the manuscripts that you receive will be so badly written, so dumb and pointless, so hard to read, that you will shake your head with incredulity at the thought of their authors actually believing that you would publish them. So it goes.

This leads us to The Rejection Slip. If you must, have some rejection slips printed to enclose with the manuscripts that you return. If you have time, though, try to give the author *some* clue as to why you are rejecting the submission. If you can't do this without being cruel, then send just the printed slip. Maybe you will like a piece but can't use it because you are

A little humor is not out of place in a rejection slip.

The material enclosed has been given careful consideration and is not suitable for use in our publication at this time.

We do, however, appreciate your interest.

The Editors.

---

december
BOX 274
WESTERN SPRINGS,
ILLINOIS 60558

Sorry, "no" on this. Thanks for sending.

EVERGREEN REVIEW, INC.
80 University Place
New York, N.Y. 10003
989-6400

Thank you for sending us your manuscript.

We've read it carefully, but have had to decide against its publication in EVERGREEN REVIEW. Many thanks, though, for letting us see it. We are returning it herewith.

THE EDITOR

P.S.: Please forgive us for this impersonal note. We'd like to comment on each manuscript, but there are far too many to make this possible.

---

overstocked at the moment or because it doesn't fit in with your style of magazine. You should note this on the rejection slip.

If you feel qualified to write a proper critique, why not do it? You might be putting some future Ernest Hemingway on the right track and he'll dedicate his first best-seller to you. Writers want to know (and don't we all?) why they have been rejected. If your comments are kind and helpful, they'll be grateful for the advice.

Because not all the submissions you receive will be usable, whenever you announce that you are looking for material make sure to stress that manuscripts unaccompanied by addressed, stamped envelopes will not be returned. (SASE—Self Addressed Stamped Envelope—is a term that most writers know.) Better keep a few 9x12 envelopes and some extra stamps around just in case. (Yes, send them back. You don't want to keep the manuscripts and the cost of returning one now and then is part of your overhead. Most writers are pretty good about including the SASE.) Manuscripts qualify for the Special Fourth Class Book Rate, so if they are heavier than two ounces, that's the way to mail them. [See Appendix]

The American Scholar   1811 Q Street, N.W. Washington, D. C. 20009

Thank you for sending us the enclosed manuscript. We have read it carefully and regret that it does not meet our editorial needs at this time.

The number of manuscripts received makes it impossible for us to offer individual comment. We would like, however, to thank you for your interest in the SCHOLAR.

THE EDITORS

Sorry we can't use this.

We are overstocked.

The Editors

NEW LETTERS
University of Missouri - Kansas City
Kansas City, Missouri 64110

CHICAGO REVIEW

THE UNIVERSITY OF CHICAGO
CHICAGO, ILLINOIS 60637

Thank you for letting us read your
manuscript. We regret that it does not
suit our needs at present.

Ed Gerson
FOR THE EDITORS
Fiction Editor

While stressing the SASE, mention also that all manuscripts must be typewritten and double-spaced. There's no reason why you should have to try to decipher somebody's childish scrawl.

You have one very important obligation when you receive manuscripts: You should read all submissions and accept them or reject them quickly. Putting this task off won't make it any easier later on.

Many editors of little mags take a cavalier attitude toward those who submit material, often holding on to it for months. This is really unfair to the poor devil in Florida or North Dakota or wherever who is checking the mailbox every day for some word from you. Don't do that to a writer.

Not only are there callous editors who will hold on to submissions, there are those who will use a piece and never even bother to notify the author that it was printed. That is low and inconsiderate.

Don Rice

Dear Editor:

Thank you for publishing your magazine. I regret that it does not fit my present needs. Your periodical was given careful consideration and the fact that I can offer no submissions at this time does not necessarily imply criticism of its merit.

Unfortunately, the large number of magazines being published does not permit time for a personal comment. I do appreciate your thinking of me and hope for your continued interest in my writing.

Sincerely,

Don Rice

The writer strikes back.

What's the Magazine to be Called

What?

There was once a joke printed in the *New Yorker* showing a woman seated at a typewriter and saying to her husband, "I'm going to write a book. What should I call it?"

It does seem silly to try to name something before it is even written, but sometimes the name can actually help you to determine the course that you are going to take. For example, if you call your magazine *The Voice of the Railroad Engineer,* this pretty much limits what you will publish. On the other hand, if you call it, *Everything Under the Sun*, there's hardly anything you *can't* publish.

Even though you may change the name when it comes time to publish the magazine, come up with a working title now. Keep in mind the sort of people you are trying to attract as readers. If you are going to publish articles by and for railroad engineers you'd best not call your periodical *Poetry for the Masses*. You can choose a literal name such as *The Journal of Modern Well Digging*, something general such as *The Northern Quarterly*, or something obscure such as *The Stagnant Gourd*, but whatever name you choose it should convey something to somebody (if only to yourself).

Beware of getting too tricky. There was once an underground newspaper entitled *Goob Yeak Gergibal.* It was failing solely because nobody could even remember the name, and the publishers finally had to change it.

How the Magazine Will Be Printed

You can't begin seriously to plan your magazine without first knowing how it is to be printed. This will determine, to a large extent, the format that your magazine will take.

For centuries, the method of reproducing a number of copies from one original meant applying ink to a raised surface, and then pressing that surface against the material on which the image was to be transferred — much like a linoleum block print.

This kind of printing is still being done, but for all practical purposes it can be disregarded by a magazine publisher. The nearly universal printing method used today is photo-offset. Unlike the mechanical process of the past, offset printing is principally a photo-chemical process.

The original copy is prepared on a flat surface and then photographed. From the resulting negative, the image is transferred to a photo-sensitive aluminum plate. After the transference, the plate is desensitized. That is, it is chemically treated so that its surface no longer responds to light shining on it. The plate is then coated with a special lacquer. The lacquer will adhere only to the exposed areas of the plate. Unlike the old raised printing plates, these are *planographic* (able to print with only a flat surface).

The offset plate is placed on the press. As it turns, a thin film of specially treated water is applied to the plate. This adheres only to the surfaces of the plate that have not been coated with lacquer. After it passes the water roller, the plate contacts an ink roller. The ink is repelled by the water and adheres only to the dry, or lacquered, portions of the plate. Next, it comes in contact with a large roller covered with a rubber "blanket" and the image is printed in reverse on this blanket.

The press has simultaneously been feeding paper

past the blanket. The image is printed by the blanket on the paper.

This process is continuous: water and ink to plate, ink from plate to blanket, ink from blanket to paper. (The offsetting of the image from plate to blanket rather than printing it directly from the plate on the paper is where the term "offset" comes from.)

This may seem as clear as mud right now, but once we have gone through the entire procedure (and once you have had some printing done) you will understand it perfectly.

There are many "quick" printers in every large city

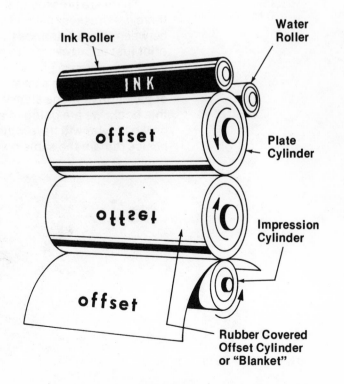

who have equipment that avoids the hassle of making metal plates. In some cases they use a copy machine to make their plates of paper. Others use a large camera with a photosensitive roll of plate material in the camera back. The copy is photographed and the finished plate ejected out the back ready to go on the press.

In neither case — copy machine or automatic plate-maker — is the quality as good as that which results from metal plates. For many jobs this difference is negligible and not worth worrying about. If you have a choice between just these two, however, choose the automatic plate-makers.

There are presses that will print postcards and there are presses that will print 96-page newspapers. In between these extremes there are presses that will print just about every size and format variation. The most popular size press, and the one to which you are more likely to have access, prints 8½ x 11-inch sheets of paper on just one side at a time. For the purposes of this book, we are going to assume that is the size press on which you will have your magazine printed. The basics remain the same no matter what the size.

The Multilith 1250.

The Magazine's Format

Since we are limited, for the purposes of this discussion, to 8½ x 11" paper, there are only two page sizes that we can reasonably use: full-sheet pages and half that size (5½ x 8½").

It might as well be mentioned here that in printing, as in most other trades, the *width* is always given first when talking about dimensions. You could, for example, fold your 8½ x 11" paper the long way if you wanted. This is sometimes done for brochures, but it isn't good for a magazine. If you did fold it the long way, your page size would be 4¼ x 11".

Using this size paper, the best page size is 5½ x 8½" because of the binding. If you use full sheets of

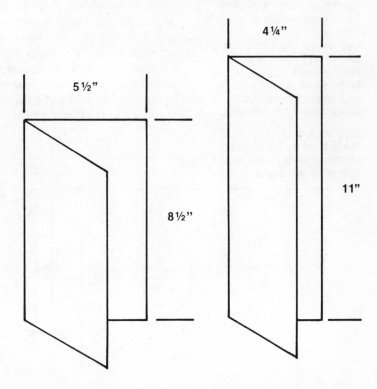

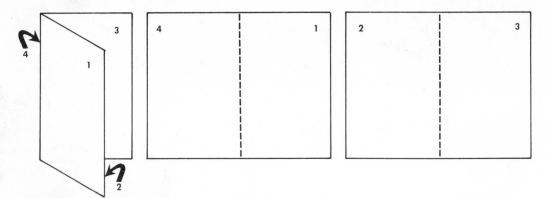

A single sheet of paper, folded in half, will provide four pages.

On the opposite page you'll see how the pages must be matched in order to have proper pagination for a **16-page booklet.**
Pages 2 and 15 will be printed on the back of the sheet on which pages 16 and 1 are printed, 4 and 13 on the back of 14 and 3, and so forth. Odd pages should always be on the right, even pages on the left. Before going too far with the planning of your magazine, make a *dummy*. Take blank pieces of paper of the size you intend to use, assemble them, and fold them in half. If you number each page, you will know which pages have to be matched when you disassemble the sheets.

Four sheets of paper, folded and collated one inside another, will make a sixteen-page booklet.

paper for pages, then in order to keep them together (which is all "binding" means) you will have to staple them along the edge. This would give your magazine a sloppy and unprofessional appearance. If you fold the sheets of paper in half, they can be stapled along the fold. This is best.

Folding them in half and then stapling on the fold does limit the number of sheets of paper you can use for this size page and still have a neat appearing magazine. Normally, you wouldn't want to go beyond 40 pages, though there's nothing to stop you from using more if you wanted.

One important thing to remember: When planning a magazine that is to be composed of folded sheets of paper, always think in terms of 4-page increments. One sheet of paper folded will make four pages so there's no way to add just one or two. If it turns out after you have all your material assembled that you have a 25-page magazine, you'll have to either eliminate one page of material or add three more (or stretch what material you have to fill three more).

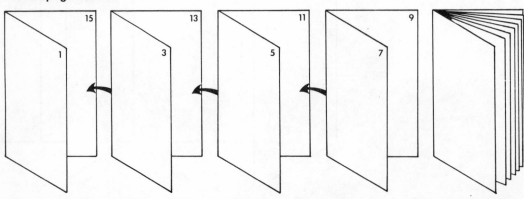

16	1

2	15

14	3

4	13

12	5

6	11

10	7

8	9

Finding and Dealing With a Printer

Before you go to the trouble of preparing copy, you ought to have a good idea of just what it will cost you to have the magazine printed.

Unless you happen to be enrolled in the graphic arts department of a school, you will probably have to go to a commerical printer. Before you talk to any printer, however, know as much as possible about what it is you want him to do. Even if you haven't entirely made up your mind about how many pages it is you intend to have, you can still get a fairly exact quote on the job.

First you must ask his price for printing (in our case) x-number of 8½x11" sheets of paper on both sides if you provide him with camera-ready copy. (More about that in the next chapter). Before you can ask that, you must decide what the "x" stands for in "x-number." In other words, how many copies of your magazine do you want?

No matter how many copies, the cost of photography and preparing the plates is going to be the same. That, in itself, is a large part of the cost of having something printed. Once it's on the press, it's just as easy to run 500 copies as it is 100 and the cost will not increase proportionately. There's no point in having fewer than 100 copies printed — you probably won't save a dime. Get two quotes: one for the minimum number of copies you would want, and another for the maximum. Be realistic about quantities: there's almost no way you are going to sell 1,000 copies.

The printer will want to know on what kind of paper you want the printing to be done. He'll suggest such mysterious things as 20-lb offset, 80-lb enamel, etc. Unless you know about such things, tell him quite frankly that you do not know. Explain to him that you haven't much money but that you would naturally want it on the best paper you can get without its costing you an arm and a leg. He'll probably end up suggesting 20-lb offset paper and will show you a sample. Take his advice. He doesn't want you to buy something more expensive than you can afford. All printers know more about trying to collect bad debts than they would care to know. In fact, he'll probably think that you are another bad debt in the making.

Let's get one thing straight: You should never order a magazine printed and expect to pay for it later with the sales revenue. If you haven't got the cash to give the printer with the order, put off publishing until you have the cash. Telling him right off the bat that you are prepared to do this—to pay him when you place the order—will make him a much more agreeable man to deal with. He might even shave a little off the price.

If you are considering using any other color ink than black, ask him what it would cost per sheet to add it. You can decide later how many sheets — if any — on which you would like to have a second or a third color.

Next, you'll want to know about cover stock. Having the cover printed on a heavier or slicker kind of paper than the pages inside will improve the appearance of your magazine.

He'll show you a variety of cover stock. White or colored index is a safe choice for a little mag, but you might want something fancier. What you use will depend entirely on your personal taste and budget.

There are other prices you will want to know: typesetting (which is usually charged by the hour and knowing the hourly rate will convey nothing to you unless you know more about it and this will be explained in the next chapter), halftone and line illustrations (next chapter) and PMT's (again, next chapter).

Knowing these costs and knowing your budgetary limitations will help you plan your magazine. It won't be an automatic decision because you may have to choose between, say, an extra color in the center spread, including a halftone illustration, or using a good cover stock, if you can't afford them all. (And maybe you can afford none.)

You could use one printer to set the type and do the necessary photography for illustrations, and then go to a "quick" printer for the printing of the magazine. The quick printers are invariably the cheaper, but they often do not have typesetting or photography equipment. Check the Yellow Pages under "Printers" to locate the quick printers.

You will also want to know what he will charge to collate, fold, and staple the magazines. "Collating" means the gathering of the printed sheets into however many it takes to make a magazine. The reason you'll want him to do this is because you haven't got a stapler that can reach in 5½" to where the staples must be applied. If, by some *unlikely* chance, you have such a stapler, you can save money by collating, folding and stapling yourself.

**A 2-page layout for 5½ x 8½"
pages.**

DESIGNING THE MAGAZINE

The Page Layout

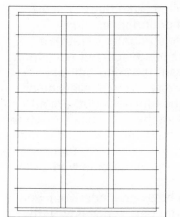

**A typical grid for an
8½ x 11" page.**

We know the size of the pages, and we know what material we are going to use. Now we have to decide what the pages are to look like. First we must determine the maximum dimensions of the area on which printed matter will appear. A good rule of thumb is to leave at least half-inch margins all around.

You must always leave at least ¼" margins for the grippers on the press to pull the paper through. If you want your printing to run off the paper (these are called "bleed pages") you must use oversize paper and then trim it to the finished size. Some presses require half-inch margins for the grippers. If you have any doubts, ask the printer what margins he requires. You will probably never go wrong if you use a half-inch.

This means, then, that we have an image area of 4½ x 7½". There's no reason why you can't get artistic and use much less. White space on a page can be as graphically attractive as type and pictures — sometimes more so.

At the top of this image area you'll want page numbers and perhaps the title of the magazine, date of publication, etc. Some magazines do this on every page. Even if you don't care to use the title of the magazine, there is *no excuse* for omitting page numbers. To do so can confuse the printer (who has to print the pages back-to-back), the collator (who must gather the pages in proper sequence), and the reader (who would like to be able to use the table of contents).

By allowing space for page numbers (called "folios") you will have reduced the amount of space on which the body copy and illustrations will be printed. When you make your layout sheets you'll have to remember to take this limitation into account.

Reproduction Film

Before you begin to gather your materials and start to paste them down, you should keep in mind the characteristics of the film that is going to be used to shoot them.

Reproduction film is called *ortho* film (from the Greek root meaning straight or upright as in *orthodontist* — the dentist who straightens teeth). It differs considerably from the *pan* black-and-white film in your camera. Pan film ("pan" meaning "all" or "everything") photographs every shade of every color you aim your camera at. Ortho film does not. For all practical purposes, it photographs just black and white or, at least, translates everything into black and white without any gray tones as with the pan film. Since the press can print in only black and white, this works out fine.

The ortho film can both help and hinder your work. For one thing, it confuses light blue and yellow with white, and it thinks that red is black. Other colors such as green and brown, for example, it might only partially photograph, not being sure just what they are. The printer can, with filters over his camera lens, trick the film into believing that certain shades of blue and other colors are black, but it *always* thinks that red is black. (This comes in handy in the darkroom: The printer can work with a red safelight and the film believes that it is in total darkness.)

Avoid colors on your paste-up except to your advantage. Since the film doesn't see blue lines, you can use them to guide you in defining the limits of the image area or in keeping pictures and type square on the page. If you have an illustration or some type you want to use that is printed in green ink, have your printer reshoot it to make a black-and-white print for the paste-up. He may not have had trouble photographing the green; then, again, he might. Best not to find out after it's all pasted up.

Setting the Type

illicit still
mammon
IBM Selectric

illicit still
mammon
IBM Executive

**The IBM Executive
typewriter spaces the
letters proportionately.
The IBM Selectric, as with
most typewriters, gives an
equal amount of space to
each letter.**

Letter Gothic

Light Italic

Courier

Courier Italic

Prestige

αβγδε{ʃ†→

Delegate

Orator

**These are just some of
the typefaces available
using just on type-
writer.**

Old Clunker

**This is what copy typed on
your old clunker will look
like if you have it
reproduced.**

By what method should the type be set? Since it's
going to be photographed when it is all done, you don't
have to depend on professional typesetting, but if you
can afford it, that's the way to go. You can, if you want,
use just about anything from hand lettering to com-
puter-set type.

The least expensive method (that is also quite
readable) is an electric typewriter with a carbon ribbon.
Carbon ribbons are for one-time use only, unlike the
reusable cloth ribbons on manual typewriters. If you
have access to such a typewriter and haven't much
money, that's the thing to use. One of the best choices
is the IBM Selectric. You'll get fairly clean type and you
can choose from among different typefaces. Another
good choice is the IBM Executive. The nice thing about
this typewriter is that it devotes a different amount of
space to each size letter and looks more like
professionally set type — but it has only one typeface.

If you have a manual typewriter that you want to
use, remember this: The finished product is going to
look no better than the original. Before you resort to
that old clunker at home, make every effort to find
something else. If you must use it, give it a good
cleaning first.

With a typewriter, you will have to choose between
justified and unjustified right-hand margins. That is,
do you want every line to be exactly the same length or
can you live with a ragged edge such as the type you're
reading? There was time when nobody — not even
publishers of church bulletins — would consider a
ragged right-hand margin, but styles change and this is
one that surely has. People finally realized that
justifying typewriter type was an arduous and useless
task.

In order to decide whether or not to use type that is
professionally set, you must know if you can afford it.
A typical manuscript (typewritten on an Elite

The type in this book, because it was set on a computer, could have been justified automatically. The decision was made to set it ragged right in order to maintain regular spacing. The computer would have taken the white space left at the end of each line and distributed it among the words in the line sometimes resulting in a lot of distracting white space.

typewriter) has approximately 250 words per page. A good typesetter can set and print approximately 25 words per minute, or one page every 10 minutes. At that speed, you can figure six typewritten pages per hour. If you know what a printer charges per hour for typesetting, you can make a ballpark estimate on what it would cost you for any particular manuscript. These times apply only to type being set on a computer typesetter and not on a Linotype machine. Not only do Linotype operators make considerably more money per hour than computer operators, they set considerably less type. Avoid them.

If you have the type set professionally, the typographer (typesetter) is going to want to know the size type you want, the typeface, and the width of the columns in which it is to be set. He may suggest Helvetica 9 on 10 in 18 pica columns. What the hell does that mean?

Helvetica is the name of the typeface. He might as easily have suggested Caledonia or Times Roman or a dozen others. Tell him what it is you are doing. Ask for his recommendation from among the typefaces that he has available. This is an area where there are many prejudices. One typographer prefers one style of type for body copy and another prefers a different style. Most printers have a feel for this, and usually you can't go too far wrong following their suggestions.

Now about those numbers: Printers use various measurements that are meaningless to anyone else — but they're not hard to learn. The basic measurement is the *pica* (sometimes called an *em*) and there are six picas to the inch. Each pica is divided into 12 *points*.

There are 72 points to the inch, but this does not mean that 72-point type is an inch high. Type is measured from the bottom of the lowest *descender* (as on the tail of the "p") to the top of the highest *ascender* (as on the top of the "l") and then a little more space is

72 pts.

Not all styles of type, even when the same size (in this case, 24-pt) take up the same amount of space.

Type **Type** Type

added to make sure that descenders and ascenders don't touch when one is on a line above another. There is considerable variation among typefaces when it comes to the length of descenders and the height of ascenders compared to the height of the lower-case letters. Therefore, one 24-point type will appear considerably larger or smaller than another.

In past years when nearly all type was set in metal, each line of type was called a *slug*. 9 on 10 simply means 9-point type on a 10-point slug. Even though metal is hardly ever melted down anymore to be cast in slugs ("hot type") the term remains. Today's computers set the type photographically directly on paper ("cold type"). You still get 9-point type on a 10-point slug even though there is no longer any such thing as a "slug." What these measurements tell you, just as they did in the days of hot type, is that there's a little extra spacing (in this example, one point) between lines.

(Apropos to this discussion, the metal from which the type was cast was mostly lead with a little tin and antimony — and maybe even a little copper. The thin strips of metal that were used for extra spacing between lines of type were called *leads*. Printers setting type on photocompositors still refer to the spacing between the lines as *leading*.)

The question remains, what size type? 9 on 10 is okay if you have a lot of material to be set but not much space to get it in. This book is set in 10-point type on a 12-point slug — a comfortable size for reading. Sometimes the size in which you have type set depends on how much room you have for it.

Can you estimate beforehand how much space a certain type-size will take? Yes. But since typefaces vary so much, there are no really good universal formulas.

It's best, until you've had quite a bit of typesetting done, just to have it set in a size that suits you. If it

Words per
Square Inch

Type Size

8 on 10	23
10 on 12	16
11 on 13	13
12 on 14	9

One very rough way to estimate the amount of space a manuscript will need when set in various type sizes.

This type (6-pt) is set in a line much too wide (34 picas) to be comfortably and easily read. It should have been set no wider than 15 picas.

This type is set in a column width much too narrow for its size. The eye has to move back and forth too quickly. Not only that, if you use any long words (such as antidisestablishmentarianism) you drive the typesetter crazy trying to figure out where to hyphenate and you thoroughly confuse the reader.

runs longer than you had hoped, go to more pages. If you can't afford more pages, leave something else out. If it runs short, use more white space or add some pictures.

If you want to continue to be a magazine publisher, you'll want to become more adept at estimating the amount of space needed to set each article or story. You will become more adept. In this skill, as in many others, you will grow with the job.

One way to decide what size typeface to use is to look at a number of books and magazines until you find something you like. Take a copy to the printer. He'll be able to tell you what size it is. The same is true with a style of typeface. Chances are he'll have something pretty close to it — and might even be able to match it exactly.

As to the column widths: Columns are invariably measured in picas. If you remember, there are six picas to the inch. Since our image area is 4½" wide (27 picas) it's too wide for two columns of type set in any size that can easily be read.

Why too wide and too narrow? A general rule to keep in mind when determining column widths is this: A column of type should be between 13 and 30 times the type size. For example, if you are using 9-point type, your column width should not exceed 22 picas, or 270 points. On the other hand, columns of 16-point type should be no *narrower* than 17 picas.

Large type set in very narrow columns is difficult to justify along the right-hand margin and is not easy to read. The reader must move too quickly from one line to the next. Very small type set in extremely wide columns is difficult to follow across the page and, in long paragraphs, it is hard to pick up the next line when the reader's eyes travel back to the left-hand margin.

If the column width you want to use is too wide for two columns on a page, or too narrow for just one, you might consider changing your page size. If you are stuck with a page width, use one column and use lots of white space.

Far too many publishers of little mags neglect to give proper consideration to the *readability* of the printed page. You want to do everything you can to make what you are publishing easy to read — at least graphically. The subject matter may be difficult to understand, but that's between the writer and the reader, with the editor acting as referee. You may be both editor *and* publisher, but don't get the two jobs mixed up. It's the publisher's responsibility to make sure that the printed matter is as accessible to the reader as possible.

Some publishers of little mags use an IBM typewriter to set their type, but then they have the type reduced photographically so that they can get as many words as possible in a single issue without going to the expense of adding more pages. They compound the problem of its readability by not taking the trouble to set it in two columns. This is unfair to both the reader and the writer. It also discourages older readers whose vision might not be perfect.

If you feel that you absolutely must use reduced size type, the least you can do is to set it in narrow columns. It's no more difficult to do this, and it makes working the type around illustrations easier when you paste up the final pages. More importantly, though, it is much easier to read tiny type set in narrow columns than it is when set in wide columns. You eyes can travel back to the beginning of the next line without getting lost along the way. Something to always keep in mind is R. Randolph Karch's Layout Rule No. 20 from his book *Printing and the Allied Trades* (New York: Pitman Publishing Company, 1958): "Above all, remember that anything printed was made to be easily read."

Headings

In addition to the body copy, you'll need type set for the various headings in your magazine. This is something that you can do yourself and produce quite professional looking work. In some cases, better than your printer can do for you.

There are many manufacturers of "transfer letters." These are letters of a wax material printed on sheets of translucent paper and need only to be rubbed into place on the finished paste-up. The reason you might be able to do a better job than your printer is that you can, with some practice and a little care, space them in a more eye-pleasing way than his equipment may permit.

You can also get these letters in typefaces that your printer hasn't available. And, unlike type that your printer can set, these can be placed directly on top of artwork. (Your printer can do this, but it is a much more complicated process than if you do it yourself.)

transfer

Transfer lettering can be applied directly on photographs.

It takes some practice before one can use transfer lettering neatly, but eventually anyone can learn.

First try
Later attempt

The top line was set with transfer lettering; the bottom with a cheap photographic headliner. Notice the inferior letter spacing of the photographically set line.

WAYWARD
WAYWARD

Advertisers Gothic
Arpad Light
Avant Garde Book
Avant Garde *Med.*
Avant Garde Bold
Bolt Bold
BUSORAMA LIGHT
BUSORAMA BOLD
Compacta
Franklin Gothic
Franklin Gothic Extra Cond
Futura Medium
Futura Medium Italic
Futura Demibold
Futura Bold
Futura Bold Italic
Grotesque No. 9
Grotesque No. 9 Italic
Grotesque No. 216
Helvetica Light
Helvetica Light Italic
Helvetica Medium
Helvetica Medium Italic
Helvetica Bold
Helvetica Bold Italic

Just a few of the many
transfer typestyles available.

There are also letters available on acetate sheets that you can cut out and press down. These are fine too, but you can't apply them directly on a photograph. The edges of the acetate show up when the pictures are printed.

The assortment of letters you get on a sheet — the number of a's, b's, c's, etc. — sometimes seems calculated to make you run out of one letter before any of the others. Then you have to invest in yet another entire sheet to get just one *t* or *c*. It's hard to anticipate everyone's needs, but some of the assortments could be selected a little more scientifically than what the manufacturers produce. Some letters are naturally in short supply, so try to stay away from headings with many x's or q's. [See Appendix]

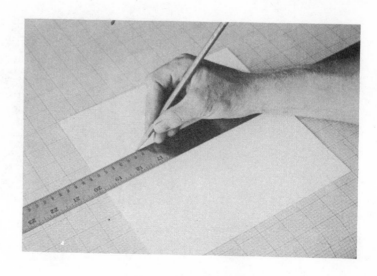

Before applying transfer
lettering, you must first
draw a guideline with a
non-reproducible blue
pencil.

Lay the sheet over the paper with the character you wish to transfer in position over your guideline. (It's best in most cases to disregard the guidelines printed on the sheets themselves—they are usually not accurate.) With a soft colored pencil (a graphite pencil might tear the backing sheet) rub the letter into place.

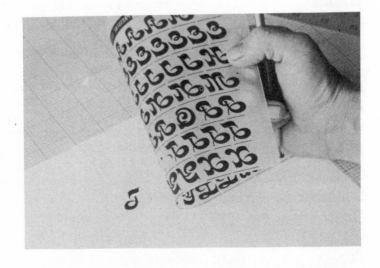

Peel back the sheet without moving it from its position to examine the letter. With many brands of lettering, the characters do not transfer cleanly.

Lay the sheet back into position and go over the parts that didn't transfer.

Examine it again. The letter may still not have transferred completely.

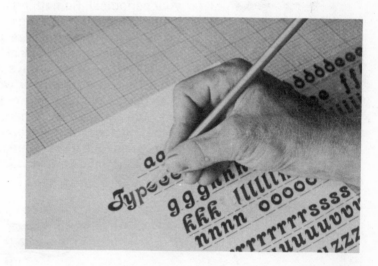

Continue this process with the rest of the needed characters.

When complete you'll have a line of professional looking type.

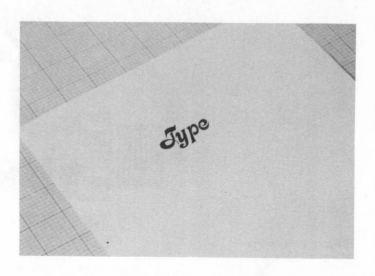

Illustrations

You'll probably want to include illustrations in your periodical. Something that hardly ever seems to happen is that the drawing or photograph you want to use is exactly the same size as you would want it to appear in the printed magazine.

Usually, but not always, you will want it smaller. It is always best to *reduce* artwork rather than to *enlarge* it. Reducing pictures also reduces their flaws and reducing photos makes them appear in better focus. Enlarging does the reverse. Some pictures such as old engravings look more interesting enlarged, flaws and all — in fact, the flaws add to the interest.

An old line engraving.

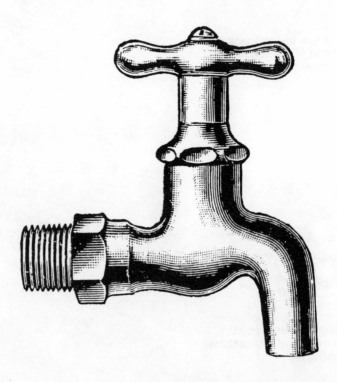

The same engraving enlarged 200%.

FINDING PROPORTIONS BY THE
ALBEBRAIC METHOD

$$\frac{A}{B} = \frac{b}{a}$$

A is to B as b is to a. The unknown dimension can be found by cross multiplication. Suppose you have an illustration that is 1½" x 2" and you want to make it 4" high. What does that do to the 1½" width?

$$\frac{1.5}{2} \times \frac{n}{4}$$

$$2n = 1.5 \times 4$$

$$2n = 6$$

$$n = \frac{6}{2}$$

$$n = 3$$

Smaller or larger, you've got the same problem: to keep the proportions in the reduction or enlargement. The best way to do this is by using a *proportioning wheel.* [See Appendix]

These are of fairly recent invention and it's surprising that it took as long as it did to invent them. If you can't get one (a proportioning wheel is one of the handiest tools a layout artist can own, so *try* to get one) you can use the algebraic method. If that's a problem you can't solve, use the diagonal line method.

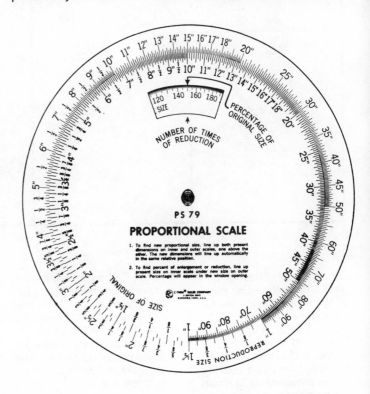

A proportion wheel. This one, reduced here, is six inches in diameter, made of plastic, and costs $2.50. Many manufacturers of graphic arts supplies give away cardboard 5½" diameter wheels. Your printer may have an old one that he can give to you.

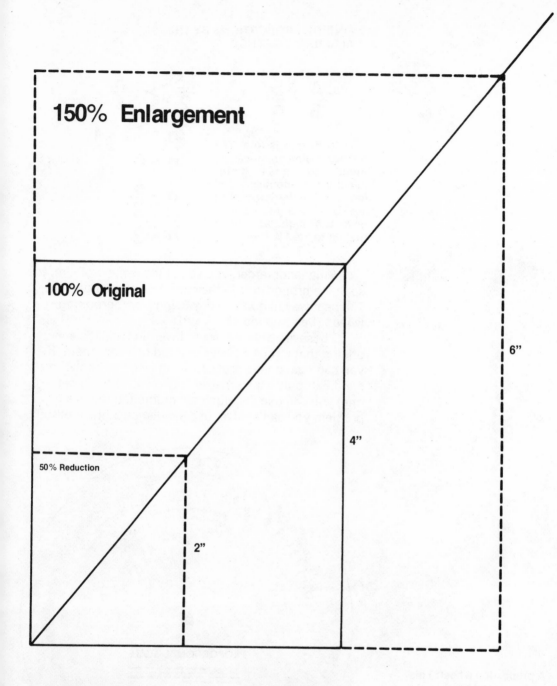

150% Enlargement

100% Original

50% Reduction

2"

4"

6"

On a separate sheet of paper, draw the exact size of the artwork you want to enlarge or reduce. Then draw a diagonal line from one corner to another. Using the bottom line (or left-hand line) as a starting point, measure up or down to the new dimension you need. Extend that line (parallel to the original) to the diagonal line. The other dimension (in this case the width) can be found automatically by drawing a perpendicular line from the juncture of the diagonal and the new line.

The cropped and reduced picture made from the original below.

You might want to use just a portion of a picture. If it's a photograph it will have to *cropped*. It's best not to cut the picture down to size, but to put crop marks right on it. Not all writing instruments will leave a legible mark on a glossy photos, so you'll have to use a special marking pen or grease pencil. [See Appendix]

Speaking of pictures, if you have to write on the back of the glossy photo, do not press down hard with a pencil or ballpoint pen. The indentations that you make might show up on the picture side and there's no way to get rid of them.

CROP   Reduce to 63%

Where to Find Illustrations

There are three sources of illustrations: 1. original art and photos; 2. stock photo services and clip art services; and 3. "borrowed" art.

Original art and photos you can solicit in the same way as you do articles and stories.

Clip art and stock photo services offer as wide a selection of illustrations as you could ever want — but you must pay for them. [See Appendix]

Borrowed art is *not* wherever you can find it. Most printed matter is copyrighted. That is, it belongs to people and those people have declared that it belongs to them and that its use is limited to whomever has permission to use it. Artwork, just like CB radios and diamond rings, is private property. It cannot be taken without permission of the owner. Unlike CB radios, however, artwork eventually does enter the public domain and anybody can use it.

A copyright now lasts for the lifetime of the copyright holder *plus* 50 years. This applies to works published after January 1, 1978. Before that time a copyright lasted for a maximum of 56 years. If you find an illustration in an old book that you want to use, check the copyright date in the front. If something was published before 1921, it is now in the public domain.

Halftone Illustrations:

Halftones (photos, paintings, airbrush drawings, wash drawings, etc.) are actually *continuous tone* pictures before being printed on a press. They have gradations in tone from white, through various densities of gray, to black.

A photograph has tiny crystals of silver nitrate in the emulsion surface of the paper that become darker as they are exposed to more and more light. They are capable of becoming any of the infinite shades of gray between the two extremes. This is fine for photos, but impossible for a printing press which is not capable of reproducing an infinite number of gray tones. If you put black ink in a printing press, it is going to print black ink on the paper. Period.

What has to be done is to transform the original photograph, with all its gray tones, into larger and smaller dots of black ink that combine with the white of the paper to give the appearance of grays.

This result is achieved by placing a dotted plastic *screen* over the film in the process camera. The dots on the screen are in a checkerboard pattern, every other dot being clear. As the image on the photograph in the copy board is focused on and exposed through this screen over the film, the dots are expanded or diminished depending on the density of light from the various parts of the photo. An extreme amount of light from a very white area of the photo wipes out the dots completely. No light at all from a black portion of the picture not only leaves the dots in, but fills in the spaces between them.

A greatly enlarged portion of the top photo on page 40 showing the dot pattern. When held at arm's length you can see the picture clearly.

A photo reproduced with a 100-line screen (100 dots to the inch). This particular screen is suitable for most purposes.

A straight-line screen.

Some screens are more suitable than others for various photos. This *mezzo* screen adds something to the mood of this particular picture that the two screens above do not. Ask your printer what screens he has available.

Process cameras can reduce art to 18-20% of the original size, and enlarge up to 250%. Ask your printer what the limits of his camera are. You will also want to know the dimensions of the copyboard that holds the work to be photographed (so that you won't give him art larger than he can shoot) and the largest size negatives or photos that he can produce.

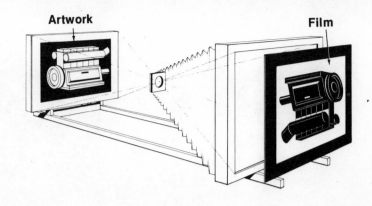

Artwork **Film**

The number of dots per linear inch on the screen determines how detailed the printed halftone picture will be. The more dots, the more detail; the fewer dots, the coarser the detail. The limit of practicable fineness is determined by the quality of printing equipment and paper used. For most offset printing, 100- to 130-line screens work fine.

You don't have to know much about this, but if you're interested in publishing you'll want to. You do have to know that photos and other continuous tone art need to be photographed separately from the printed type. They have to be *screened*. After the page negatives are shot (photographed) the screened half-tones must be *stripped-in*. The printer will cut a hole in the page neg the size of the half-tone and then tape the half-tone into place.

You can make this job easier for him (and guarantee the positioning of the halftone) if you paste a black "window" on the page where you want the picture to go. Remember that on a negative the blacks and whites are reversed. A black square on the paste-up will be a clear window on the negative. Make this window at least an eighth-inch larger all around than

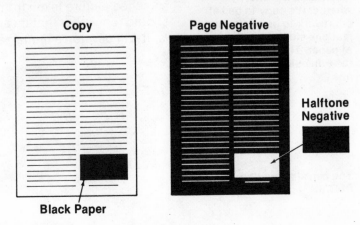

Copy **Page Negative**

Halftone Negative

Black Paper

PMT's can be pasted right on the original page copy.

NOTE: When you make your final paste-up, use just one side of each sheet of paper. Don't paste it up on both sides the way it is going to be printed. In fact, when giving any material to a printer, whether it's copy to be set or artwork to be shot, use just one side of each sheet of paper. The material on the other side could be missed.

you'll want the finished picture to be. This will leave the printer space for taping the picture in. He will use the crop marks on the photo to line up the portion of the picture that you want to appear in the window.

There's another way to include halftones without stripping-in the negatives. This is the *copydot* method. You simply paste down pre-screened prints directly on the page. The finished product isn't going to be as good as a stripped-in neg because some of the dots are so tiny they won't be photographed. This is especially true of halftones that you have taken from another printed page.

One copydot method that is usually quite acceptable is the pasting down of PMT's. The photographer shoots special prints for this purpose. (The initials PMT stand for Photo Mechanical Transfer.) Not all printers have the equipment to do this. Ask your printer if he does. It's usually cheaper than using stripped-in negs and gives you the advantage of seeing in advance what the printed page will look like. It also permits you to overlap pictures — something that is more difficult to do with stripping-in

If you must, for some reason, use a previously screened picture taken from another source, you should remember that it can't be screened again. If it is, it will develop a *moire* pattern and this looks dumb.

You can also overlap PMT's.

(Actually, it is possible to rescreen pictures and avoid the moire pattern. Most printers know how to do this, but there are some who don't — or simply won't.) Used intentionally, you can produce some very interesting graphic effects with moire patterns.

Keep in mind that no matter how your pictures are reproduced — copydot from PMT's and other printed matter, rescreened, or even stripped-in — you are going to lose some quality compared to the original. Therefore, you should choose the sharpest, most *contrasty* pictures you can. ("Contrasty" is photographer's jargon for a wide range between the darkest portion of a picture and the lightest.) It could be that for some particular effect you want a picture of low contrast. That's fine, but low contrast pictures should be used because you want them and not because you didn't know enough to use a better picture.

If you're into photography, you already know about contrast and photo quality. If not, you might want to read up on it. [See Appendix]

This is a moire pattern caused by the improper rescreening of a previously screened photo.

A silhouette made from an outline mask.

Outline Halftones:

There are occasions when you will not want the entire picture but just an irregular shape from within it. If you are using PMT's you can cut out what you want — especially if it has a lot of straight edges. But if what you want has a lot of detail in the edges, you should make a film overlay.

Cutting the film takes a little practice, but nearly anyone can become adept with a little practice.

Another method of producing outline halftones is by *opaqueing* the negative. Opaqueing material is a very dense water color paint that will adhere to the film. It is painted over the areas of the negative that you do not wish to be printed on the page. One disadvantage of using opaque is that it is difficult to get good straight lines using a small brush. This can be solved by using pieces of *red lithographer's tape* that all printers have.

The overlay film is available in a number of shades ranging from deep ruby to bright orange. The orange is best to use because you can see through it to know exactly where you are cutting. [See Appendix]

Tape a piece of film (dull side up) over the photo you want to outline.

With an X-acto knife score two parallel lines along the top of the film. You will then be able to peel off a thin strip of the film from its clear acetate base. Do the same to the bottom.

Then cut around the portion of the picture you wish to outline.

As you go along you will
be able to peel off un-
wanted pieces of film.

Eventually, you will have
the entire outline cut.

Look for areas within the
outline that should also be
cut out.

Use the point of your knife
to separate the film from
the base sheet.

Carefully peel these off.

Give the entire picture,
mask and all, to the printer.
He will take it from there.

Line Illustrations:

These are drawings, etchings, photos, and so on that are composed of just black and white areas. They have no variations of gray, but it is possible to give them that appearance depending on how the illustrations are rendered.

Line drawings can be pasted right on the layout along with the type. All you need to remember is that they should have sharp, clean lines and that they be either black or red in order to photograph well.

It is possible to make a line shot from a continuous tone photo. This is called the line-tone process. [See the review of the Kodak publication *More Special Effects for Reproduction* on page 93 of this book.]

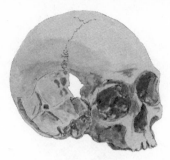

The above is a wash
drawing that had to be
screened in order to be
reproduced. But there are
various ways to produce a
halftone effect with line
renderings. Top right:
stipple technique using a
crowquill pen. Middle:
Duotone paper is
chemically treated so that
the application of one fluid
brings out lines running in
one direction and, for
darker tones, a second
fluid brings out per-
pendicular lines. Black
areas are achieved by
simply brushing on India
ink. Bottom: There are
many densities of textured
film available that can be
cut out and applied directly
on artwork. Again, black
areas are achieved with
India ink.

Designing the Cover

There are four elements that should be included in the front cover of every magazine: 1. the name, prominent and readable; 2. the price; 3. the date of issue and number; 4. cover illustration.

The Name:
The name of a magazine is similar to the logo, or trademark, of a corporation. Give some thought to the type style in which it will be set and to any other decorative artwork that will regularly accompany it on the cover. If you can, try to convey something about the magazine's style and content. *Don't get hung up on this.* A great deal of time and money is wasted designing logos that look like everybody else's anyway. The main criteria of a logo is that it be distinctive and easily read.

The Price:
If you plan on putting your magazine on newsstands or in bookstores, make sure that the price is quite obvious. People hesitate taking something to the cash register that has no price on it. They don't want to be put on the spot if the price is higher than they thought it would be.

Date of Issue and Number:
Always put a date on your magazine even if it's something as vague as a season (Winter Issue, Summer Issue). And make sure to include the year. The magazine should also be numbered. There are two ways to do this: you can use *whole numbers* or *volume and number*. Whole number means that the first issue is No. 1, the second issue is No. 2, and so on. Volume and number means that you publish one volume over a pre-determined period of time and then number the

The Lower Case Plague: The designers of these barely distinguishable logos all thought they had original and clever ideas. Though none are magazine titles (some *are* publishers' logos) they illustrate the danger in trying to be cute and contemporary rather than straightforward and readable.

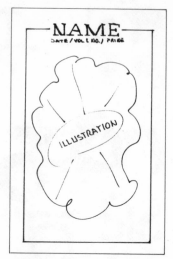

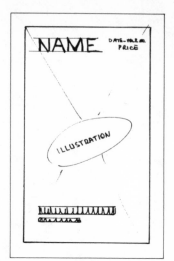

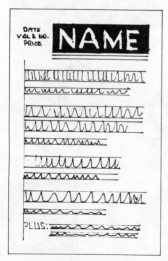

issues within each volume. Normally, a volume extends over a year. (A notable exception to this is *Mad* which is still working on the first volume and has numbers running into the hundreds.) The first issue of your magazine would be Vol. I, No. 1. Traditionally, the volume is given in Roman numerals and the number in Arabic numerals, but it isn't written anywhere that you must do it that way.

Some periodicals use both whole number *and* volume and number: Vol XX, No. 11 — Whole Number 251. Use whatever system appeals to you, but use something. Librarians, especially, become confused by un-numbered, un-dated periodicals. It goes against everything they've been taught in library school.

Cover Illustration:

You don't have to have an illustration, but there should be some invitation to the reader to open up the magazine. It could be an illustration, it could be the table of contents, it could be many things. Some periodicals use exactly the same cover for every issue, changing only the color of the cover stock or ink. Do this if you want, but look around and you'll see that the most successful magazines try to attract the attention of prospective readers by changing with every issue.

Even if you sell only by subscription and don't use any retail sales at all, you're bound to have some library subscriptions. Even though library patrons aren't buying your magazine, you still want to attract their attention. A magazine on the library shelves that goes unread issue after issue is not a good candidate to have its subscription renewed.

Layout Aids [See Appendix]

Border Tapes:

You might consider having a roll or two or three of varying widths and designs. These are the quickest way to do the job.

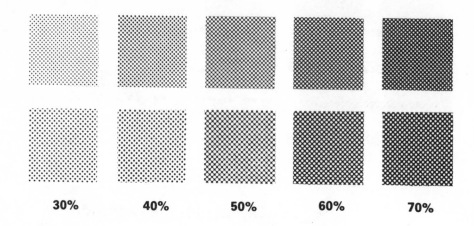

30%   **40%**   **50%**   **60%**   **70%**

Benday Shading Film:
     There was a printer named Benjamin Day who gave his name to these screens. They are a mechanical method of producing shaded backgrounds of other tonal values. Dozens of patterns are available, and they can be bought in either lift-off or transfer sheets. (Lift-off screens are better.) You can even buy the screens in pre-designed shapes such as circles and explosions. They can be used for providing a variety in layouts by incorporating them in an illustration or for color backgrounds for overprinting.

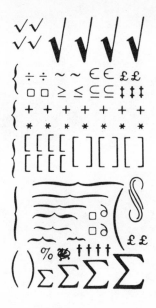

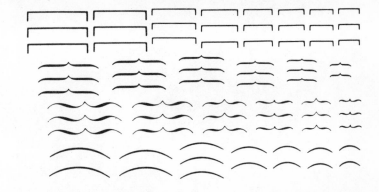

Symbol Sheets:

There are sheets of everything from data flow chart symbols to arrows to circles to chemical symbols. These are available in either transfer or lift-off sheets.

Clear Acetate:
Useful for making overlays.

Outline films:
In addition to being used for cutting outline halftones, these can be used similarly to benday sheets for making areas of solid color.

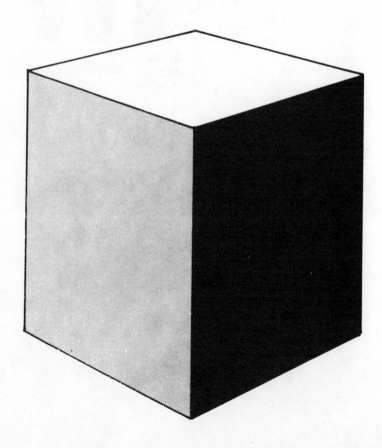

Tools for the Graphic Artist [See Appendix]

X-Acto Knife:
Everyone knows what an X-Acto knife is. You'll want to have one to cut paper, overlays and benday films, and also for moving things around on the layout: for holding tiny bits of paper before placing them down and for lifting up pasted-down items that you want to move. A difficult tool to do without. Make sure you have one. The best blade for your purposes is the No. 16.

Olfa Knife:
Nearly as good, and considerably less expensive than an X-Acto. A strip of blades is inserted into the handle of the knife. As one blade gets dull, it can be snapped off and the next one moved into place. The cost of each blade is just a tiny fraction of what an X-Acto blade costs.

Mat Knife:
Not used nearly as often as an X-Acto or Olfa, but much better for cutting heavy stock — something that you'll have to do every now and then.

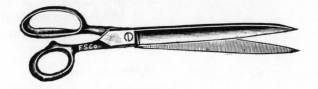

Scissors:
You've got to have them.

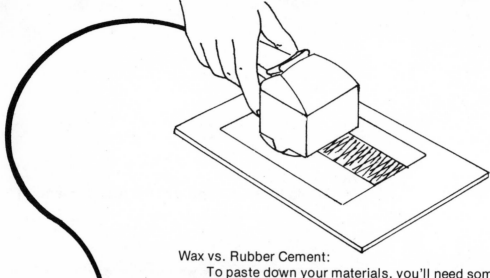

Wax vs. Rubber Cement:

To paste down your materials, you'll need some sort of adhesive. It's possible to do this job using just Scotch Magic Transparent Tape (the non-shiny kind in the green package). For a neater job you'll want to use either wax or rubber cement.

It used to be that rubber cement was the universal means of pasting down artwork, but today nearly all commercial artists and printers use wax. Problem is, you can't go down to the office supply store and buy a bottle of wax the way you can buy rubber cement. You've got to have a *waxer.* These can cost in the many hundreds of dollars, but a little hand-held job goes for around $30. If you plan on being in business for any length of time, you'll probably want one of these.

The big advantage with wax is that you can paste something down, then change your mind and put it somewhere else. Unlike rubber cement it doesn't dry up on you in the jar. You can also cover more square inches per dollar with wax than with rubber cement.

Straight-edges:

Metal rulers are best; and if you have one with inches on one edge and picas on the other, so much the better.

Alignment Rule:

To check if a paste-up has been laid down straight rather than just "eyeballing" it, you can place this transparent rule that has lines printed on it right over the copy and see immediately if everything is lined up.

Ruling Pens:
   Modern ruling pens, unlike the old fashioned kind, are simple to use. But they are expensive. If you haven't much line drawing to do, buy a felt-tip instead. As long as it's new, you'll get good sharp lines. (If you buy one, get a decent brand and not an underpriced piece of trash from the 5 & 10. The ink won't flow at a regular rate from a cheap pen, and you'll end up with sloppy lines.)

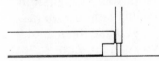

Ink from the pen will dribble under the edge of a triangle.

Triangles:
   A clear plastic triangle always comes in handy. If you plan on using it to guide you in drawing lines (they're better for this purpose than a metal ruler because you can see through them) get one with the bottom edge inset to get it away from the paper. This feature will prevent the ink from dribbling underneath. If you have a triangle without the inset edges and don't want to buy one, you can get the same effect by taping pennies here and there on the botton. Wash them with soap and water every now and then. One caution: *Never* use them as straight edges for cutting — you'll end up cutting into your triangles and they won't be straight edges anymore.

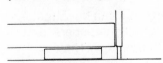

An inset bottom edge will prevent dribbling.

A penny taped to the bottom will prevent dribbling.

Templates:
   These are pieces of plastic with holes cut in them to use as guides for drawing circles, ellipses and just about everything else. They are useful (especially the circle template) but expensive and not absolutely necessary to own unless you have some very special needs. You can always find something around the house to act as a guide for circles.

India Ink and Brush:

Must-have items. You'll need to touch up pin-holes and other flaws in artwork and sometimes in transfer lettering. Spend a couple of bucks and get a good sable brush. Cheap brushes are worse than useless.

Non-reproducing Blue Pencil:

These pencils mark with a color that the film does not see but that you can. There are many times you'll be glad you had one. Almost any blue pencil will work, but if it's too deep a blue, you'll have to write very lightly to prevent its being photographed.

Layout Sheets:

You can prepare your own with a blue pencil. If you do much work you'll want some pre-printed sheets. These are pieces of heavy white stock with light blue lines on them. You can either design your own custom sheets and have your printer produce them for you (a printer might do this for nothing if you use them a lot and he gets all the business) or you can buy commerical paste-up grids.

Other Items:

There are all kinds of gadgets you can buy: light tables, edge trimmers, electric pencil sharpeners, and so on. Don't worry about these things now. They're expensive and unnecessary. If the day ever comes when you turn pro, you'll find out all about them.

FINDING READERS

So. You have a magazine. It's filled with stories and pictures and poetry. There are 500 copies of the magazine stacked here and there around the living room.

Now we must ask the burning question: Who wants to read it? Even more burning is the question: Who wants to *pay* to read it? A few friends and relatives maybe — and even they might not actually want to *read* it but will buy a copy to help you out.

The magazine looks good to you because it's your creation, and it looks good to your mother because you are her creation. Beyond that, is it of any real significance to anyone?

Ask yourself: Would you pay 50¢ or $1 or more for a home-made collection of amateur poetry? Would you really? When was the last time you bought a little mag published by people who were strangers to you? Have you ever? Does anyone?

There *are* successful little mags. In a few cases, there are some that provide a limited income for their editors and publishers and even a little for the authors. Many university quarterlies have paid editors, but these mags are invariably subsidized by the university and by grants. They couldn't survive and also pay salaries with just their subscription and advertising revenue. Little mags generally are labors of love, or tributes to the ego, providing their publishers with no more than the satisfaction of having printed them, usually at a financial loss.

Who Will Subscribe?

Your highest goal in publishing your magazine — other than its being an artistic triumph — ought to be to break even financially. This is no easy goal. To reach it you will need a list of paid subscribers. Libraries (and as many friends as you have) are your best bets to meet this need at first.

Any given county in the United States has a half-dozen libraries and, depending on where you live, as many as 25 or 50. There are public libraries, and there are also libraries in colleges, universities, and high schools. The librarians who run these places may be no more in the habit of subscribing to unknown periodicals than you are. But, after all, your magazine is locally published and the local librarians have a limited obligation to encourage that sort of activity in their own community. Go to them. Give them that sales pitch. Tell them about the local writers and artists and poets who are going to have their work published in your magazine if only they will help by subscribing.

Unless you have published something so patently offensive or so poorly done that it embarrasses people, they will probably find $2 or $5 somewhere in their budget for a year's subscription. And if you continue to publish on a more or less regular basis, they will continue to subscribe.

Libraries provide the only steady support that many little mags will ever have. They should be your first major target.

Overcoming Inertia:

It isn't the cost of the subscription that prevents libraries from getting your magazine, it's the cost of overcoming their own inertia; of processing the paperwork; of moving all the existing periodicals over one notch to fit your magazine into alphabetical order.

As everyone knows — or should know — inertia is the tendency of a body to remain in an existing state of rest or motion unless acted on by an external force. Overcoming inertia is the greatest problem you will face when trying to get libraries to subscribe. The local library does not now subscribe to your magazine and will continue to remain in this motionless state until you, the external force, act upon them and make them move.

Then, Inertia the Great Enemy, becomes Inertia the Great Friend. Once libraries subscribe to your magazine, they will continue to do so—unless you act upon them again in some adverse way (such as publishing a bad magazine) that alters their state of motion.

Promoting the Magazine

Direct-Mail Advertising:

It would hardly pay to travel around the country meeting face-to-face with librarians trying to get them to subscribe. The best way to reach out-of-town libraries is by direct-mail.

Newspapers have succeeded in persuading people that this sort of advertising is "junk mail;" that is to say, "Worthless." Don't you believe it. Newspapers, television and mass-circulation magazines want people to regard direct-mail as junk only because it is a competing advertising medium that is unable to strike back (in the same way that they attack billboards).

The fact is, direct-mail is a multi-million dollar industry that—unlike newspapers—actually pays its way at the post office. Many companies use direct-mail to solicit all their sales. If it were "junk" they couldn't do so. This isn't to say that a lot of it isn't junk, but your advertising *can't* be. If it is, you'll fail.

Look at it this way: You are selling a printed product (your magazine) to someone at a distant point. Up until a librarian reads your mailing piece (another printed product that you have published) he or she has probably never heard of you. All that is known about you is that you are selling a printed magazine. Now suppose that your mailing piece is sloppy, poorly organized, and hard to read. What judgments do you suppose a librarian is going to make about your magazine? Exactly. The librarian is going to assume that your magazine is sloppy, poorly printed, and hard to read. On the other hand, suppose that your mailing piece is nicely printed, clever, and interesting. You get the point.

Bob Stone, a very successful mail-order executive, once published the following checklist in *Advertising Age:*

CREATIVE CHECKLIST FOR DIRECT MAIL*

1. Do you have a good proposition?
2. Do you have a good offer?
3. Does your outside envelope select the prospect?
4. Does your outside envelope put your best foot forward?
5. Does your outside envelope provide reading motivation?
6. Does your copy provide instant orientation?
7. Does your mailing visually reinforce the message?
8. Does it employ readable typography?
9. Is it written in readable, concrete language?
10. Is it personal?
11. Does it strike a responsive chord?
12. Is it dramatic?
13. Does it talk in the language of life, not "advertise at?"
14. Is it credible?
15. Is it structured?
16. Does it leave no stone unturned?
17. Does it present an ultimate benefit?
18. Are details presented as advantages?

*Reprinted with permission from the September 11, 1967 issue of Advertising Age. Copyright 1967 by Crain Communications Inc.

19. Does it use, if possible, the power of disinterestedness?
20. Does it use, if possible, the power of negative selling?
21. Does it touch on the reader's deepest relevant daydreams?
22. Does it use subtle flattery?
23. Does it prove and dramatize the value?
24. Does it provide strong assurance of satisfaction?
25. Does it repeat key points?
26. Is it backed by authority?
27. Does it give a reason for immediate response?
28. Do you make it easy to order?

When you have designed your mailing piece, ask yourself every one of those questions and answer them honestly. You can fool yourself, but not your potential subscribers. They will not respond favorably to a piece of junk mail, and you're going to be wasting your money if that's what you send them.

Mailing Lists:
After you have produced your whiz-bang, sure-sell mailing piece, you have somehow to get it into the hands of librarians (or whomever). What you need now are good mailing lists. One of the best sources is your local library.

Colleges and universities are your best prospects for subscribers because they have a broader periodicals selection than public libraries and are willing to take more chances with unknown periodicals. Your local public library probably has a copy of *Lovejoy's College Guide*. In there, listed by state, are all the colleges and universities in the United States. Since *Lovejoy's* is usually in the reference section, you can't take the book home, But you can copy the addresses. For that matter, there's no reason why you can't buy your own copy and work at home. [See Appendix]

If you haven't the time or the inclination to type all those addresses yourself, you can buy them already on labels.

If you want to go after public libraries, all of their addresses can be found in *The American Library Directory* which is available in most large libraries. [See Appendix] For a list already on labels you should look into Fritz Hofheimer's list of the 1,000 largest main public libraries. [See Appendix] Larger libraries are just naturally better prospects than smaller libraries.

If your magazine has a very narrow appeal, you'd best forget libraries (except in very large cities and large universities with special collections) and concentrate on finding lists of individuals with that same narrow interest. For example, if you publish a magazine for railroad engineers, you can buy Hofheimer's list of 1,474 railroad engineers. There are many companies who sell nothing but mailing lists. These are called "list brokers." Often, they will sell only a minimum of 10,000 addresses. That's going to be more than you can afford. You can also check the latest edition of *Direct Mail List Rates and Data*. In there are listed over 27,000 mailing lists.

It should be remembered when buying a list that you are really just renting it. A mailing list can be a valuable piece of property, and its unauthorized use is no different from stealing a car. Almost any list you rent is for one-time use only. To catch those who make copies of a list and use it over, the owners always include a few "ringers." These are names that appear only on that list and if they receive any mail other than that which has been authorized, they know that the list has been used illegally.

Another good source of mailing lists is the *Encyclopedia of Associations* (available in most libraries). The associations are arranged by categories. Find your category, see what associations exist there, and write to them. Tell them what it is you are planning to do, and ask if they would care to rent you their mailing list. They might, and then again they might not. Some will, some won't. But if they do, they'll want to see a copy of what it is you would like to mail out to their membership.

Most companies that sell mailing lists offer them on three different kinds of labels: gummed, self-stick, and cheshire. The gummed labels usually sell for no extra cost on top of the basic price. Self-stick, because they are printed on more expensive stock, usually cost a little more. Cheshire lables usually sell at the basic price, but require special equipment for their application that you do not own.

The Mailing Envelope:

Once you have chosen a list and have your mailing piece designed, look again at points 3 through 5 on Bob Stone's checklist. Does your mailing envelope really do the trick? If your mailing piece is intended for railroad engineers it ought to have a picture of a railroad engine along with the words "ATTENTION, RAILROAD ENGINEERS!" or something like that. By the same token, that is not the envelope in which you enclose the piece when mailing it to librarians. This all sounds very obvious, but it is a common-sense piece of advice that is disregarded over and over.

The reason for selecting the prospect on the outer envelope is that most direct-mail advertising is never read. Most newspaper ads aren't read by everyone who reads the paper. What every advertiser is trying to do is to attract those souls who are likely to buy — the rest don't matter. And this is what you must do.

One problem is that you are not the only person trying to get the librarian to subscribe to a magazine. Nor are you the only person trying to get railroad engineers to part with their money. We are barraged with advertising from the minute we get up in the morning until we fall asleep at night. Estimates have the number of ads to which the average person is exposed daily up in the thousands.

Your mission, should you accept it — and it is almost impossible — is to have your ad be one of the very few that is noted that day and then acted on. That is why the outside envelope is so important.

You can be fairly certain that if a railroad engineer gets an envelope in the mail that says, "ATTENTION, RAILROAD ENGINEERS!" that he is going to take a look at what is inside. After that, if your magazine is worthwhile, and it's priced right, and if your mailing piece does a good job of convincing railroad engineers why it would be to their advantage to subscribe, well, you might have a so-so chance of survival.

You can see why it is extremely unlikely that a magazine of amateur poetry is going to be a success. Who's going to subscribe to it? Where would you find good prospects? How would you attract them?

Rate of return:

With high recommendations, a good mailer, and a selective mailing list, you might reasonably expect anywhere from a 1% to 5% return from those who are sent your mailing piece. Then again, you might get .025% or 10%. There is no way to know in advance. Advertisers who are planning huge mailings try a sample mailing first.

Before you have the mailing pieces printed, go through the following procedure. First, find out exactly what the mailing will cost: printing, envelopes, mailing list, and postage. Then figure out what rate of return you'll need to make a profit.

Suppose that you are sending out a thousand pieces and the total cost for putting them in the mail is $180. A subscription to your magazine is $4 a year. If only 1% respond then you will receive only $40. (1% of 1,000 = 10 x $4 = $40.)

In order to get back the money that you paid for the mailing, you must have a 4½% return (45 x $4 = $180). That's a pretty high rate of return, but let's suppose you get it. Now you are obliged to print and mail copies of your magazine to 45 subscribers for a whole year — and the money that they paid you went to pay for the cost of the mailing. So how are you ahead?

If you plan on being in business for some time and can afford to go into the hole the first year, perhaps you can get away with it. A percentage of those 45 (or 450 or 4,500) will renew their subscriptions. The renewals should cost you only a fraction of what the original subscriptions cost. If a high enough percentage renews for the second year, you can make some money. This is assuming that you have charged enough for a subscription in the first place.

Retail Sales:

You can sell a few copies in book stores and newsstands. None of the managers of these establishments are interested in your magazine, but you can probably talk the local newstand or college book store into carrying it.

You leave 10 copies with the man, and when the next issue comes out you leave 10 more. He pays you probably 60% of the retail price (get that worked out and agreed upon beforehand) for the copies that have been sold. If it's a 50¢ magazine and he sells three copies, he'll make a big 60¢ for his efforts. See why he's not interested? But if it's a small town, he'll probably carry it just as a favor to you.

There are a hundred or so bookstores around the country that make a point of carrying little mags. Many are known to forget to pay for the copies they sell. Best not to fool around with them.

You can make retail sales yourself. You take an armload of magazines and hawk them on street corners. This way, at least, you get all the money, and it's just possible that you'll sell 10 copies in an afternoon.

Magazine Advertising:

This is expensive. Even classified ads in magazines such as *Harper's* or *The Nation* cost quite a bit. A quarter-page ad costs a small fortune, and a full-page ad is out of the question. Unless you find another highly specialized journal in which to advertise, or unless you have a unique and beautiful idea for a periodical, you might as well save your money.

Periodical Displays:

Every state has a State Library Association — and they all have conferences and meetings. The American Library Asociation also has conferences, some of them regional, some national. At these conferences, the librarians have meetings and workshops and speeches and dinners and cocktail hours and all the other traditional convention activities. Much of the convention, though, is centered on a room, or huge suite of meeting rooms, in which those who sell books and magazines and library supplies have set up displays. The cost of renting the display space is incredibly high, and only the larger publishers and manufacturers can reasonably afford it.

In order that smaller publishers can participate, there are companies that rent large spaces and then sell it off in tiny bits to many different companies. For a fee, you can have your magazine displayed, along with dozens of others, on racks in a collective display. Maybe a librarian will see your magazine there. Maybe the librarian will remember the name. Maybe the librarian will even subscribe. But more than likely, none of this will happen.

If it makes you feel good to know that your periodical is on display at the National Summer Conference of the American Library Association at which there will be thousands of librarians from all over the United States, then do it. But don't expect many — if any — subscriptions as a result.

Subscription Agencies

Anywhere from one-third to one-half of your library subscriptions will come through subscription agencies. The larger, more successful agencies are huge computer operations that can handle thousands of subscriptions much more efficiently than the libraries themselves.

Basically, the service they offer to a library is this: The librarian submits a list to the agency of all the magazines that the library receives. The agency, in turn, places all the individual subscriptions and encloses a check with each order or group of orders to one magazine. This last is very important because it relieves the periodicals of the necessity of sending out invoices. The agency then sends just one bill for all the subscriptions to the librarian. This arrangement saves the librarian a lot of trouble and doesn't cost the library a penny extra for the magazines.

So where does the agency make its profit? From the magazines. Most of them will give the agencies 10-30% of the subscription price as a commission. They don't have to give them a dime, but they do. Getting just one check with each group of orders is easily worth a commission to large circulation magazines. Because the agencies have participated in the subscription process, the force of inertia is much stronger. The percentage of renewals among libraries that subscribe through agencies is considerably higher than among those that don't.

Since a little mag is such a marginal operation, there's no need to give much more than a 10-15% commission. The agency has promised the librarian that it will handle *all* subscriptions, even including those who don't pay commissions. Since agencies have very little influence over periodical selection in libraries, you needn't pay any commission at all if you don't care to. [See Appendix]

Addressing Mail Subscriptions

Many little mags put the addresses on by hand. If you have more than a couple of hundred subscribers and if you publish more than four times a year, you might want to invest in some sort of addressing equipment. [See Appendix]

Elliott Addresserette:

The Addresserette has been phased out by the Elliott Corporation. As a result, you can usually buy one reasonably cheap from a company that sells used equipment. If you do, you'd better buy enough stencils to last a lifetime because the day will come when you can no longer buy that size (Elliott still makes larger sizes for the bigger machines).

The stencils themselves are similar to mimeograph stencils in little cardboard frames. You put the address on them with a typewriter. This requires a special holder that you must get when you buy the machine — along with a special dampening device. These items are inexpensive.

Elliott's larger machines cost more than you will be willing to lay out until you have a fairly large circulation.

A-M Addressograph:

You won't want to buy — at least not right away — one of the big machines that A-M manufactures, but you may be able to find a small used manual machine for not too much. The plates are metal and require a special machine to stamp them with addresses. You will *not* find one of these at a reasonable price, but in every big city, and many smaller ones, there are companies that offer this stamping service.

This is not a cheap way to do your addressing. You have to buy metal plates, you have to pay to have them stamped, and you have to buy metal frames in which to put them.

Mini-Master:

This is one of the best methods for little mags. The equipment isn't outrageously priced and the plates

Build Your Own Mail Bag Holder

If you have a few hundred subscribers or send out lots of direct mail pieces, you'll want to use sacks provided by the Postal Service to bag your mail. (Ask for No. 2 sacks and keep the weight in each sack between 35 and 50 pounds.) Because the sacks are made of canvas they are limp and very frustrating to fill without a frame to hold them open. You can buy commercially manufactured frames but they are expensive. It's cheaper to make your own out of 2x2's.

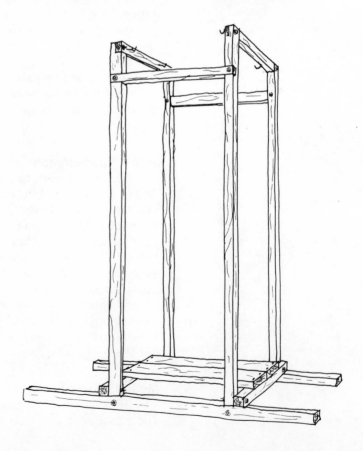

You can buy hooks at any
hardward store to screw
into the top of the frame.
The eyes around the tops of
the sacks will slip over the
hooks, but you'll want to
hacksaw off the points
first. It's easier to do this
after you have screwed
them in.

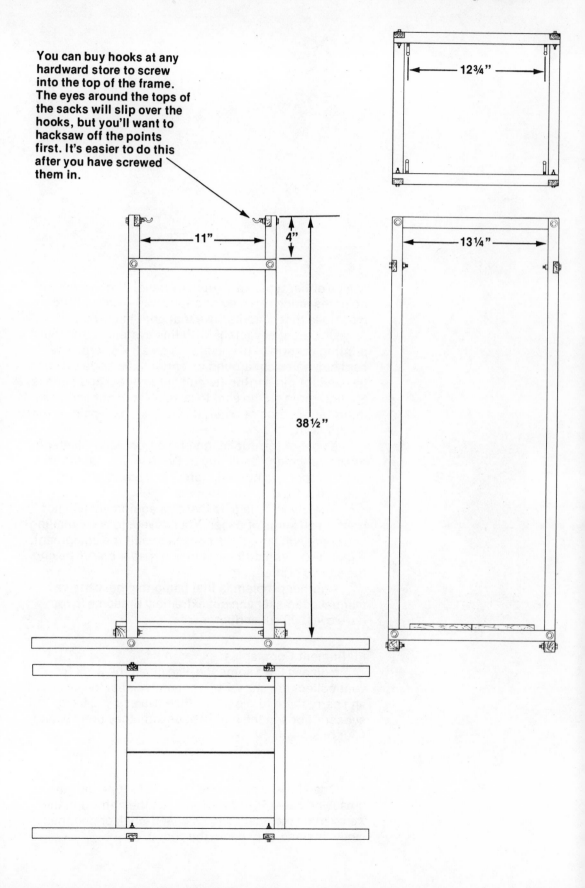

12¾"

11"

4"

38½"

13¼"

can be either typed or written by hand. The system operates much like a spirit duplicator — those little machines that schools have that print in purple.

One great advantage with this system is that the printing portion of the "plate" is on a 3 x 5 card. The card has holes cut around its entire outer edge that can be used for pin sorting (to cull out expires) and there is enough room on the card to keep all your subscription information: date of order, date billed, date paid — that sort of stuff.

The cost of the duplicating fluid from Mini-Master is priced very high. Don't buy it. Go to your local office supply store and buy a gallon of any brand of spirit duplicator fluid. It will work just fine.

One disadvantage is that this equipment will not print on all kinds of paper. Your cover stock (or mailing envelope) will have to be chosen to suit the equipment. Experiment with different kinds of paper before having the covers printed.

Another problem is that using the inexpensive manual addresser can get extremely tiresome if you have over 500 subscribers.

Fulfillment Companies:
You can have someone else do all the work for you: collect the subscription money, label the issues, and carry them to the post office. Unless you have subscriptions in the many thousands they don't want your business.

Xerox:
One of the simplest methods is to type the addresses on sheets of paper and run them through the Xerox machine using sheets of self-stick or gummed labels instead of paper in the copier.

If your mail circulation is relatively stable, this is the cheapest way to get labels without any capital outlay. But if you have many address changes or additions it's next to impossible. There's no way you can add an address in ZIP sequence—and you must do this if you use 2nd or 3rd class mail.

Renewal Notices

Make it easy. Shortly before or after sending the final issue of a subscription, send each expire a renewal notice (with some "sell" in it) and a business-reply renewal card. [See Appendix]

Be sure that the subscribers' names are already typed or otherwise printed on these cards. All they have to do is sign them and mail them back. If you can afford it, also include a postage paid envelope so that they can enclose a check with the renewal. This will save you the expense of invoicing them and it might cut down on the deadbeat list.

If you mail your magazine in an envelope, enclose the renewal notice and card with the final issue. Give them a month or so to renew, then send a follow-up notice (again, enclosing the business-reply card and envelope).

Getting Paid

You might as well plan right from the start on not getting any salary. What we're talking about here is getting paid for the subscriptions.

Libraries are almost always good for the money. Individuals, on the other hand, are less likely to pay you. They'll pay their subscription money to *Newsweek*, but they might not take your efforts

☐ **Bill me***
☐ **Bill my company***
☐ **Check enclosed**

*Your subscription will commence
with first available issue
after receipt of payment

**Take a hint from those who
should know.** *FOLIO: The
Magazine for Magazine
Management* **will not send
even one issue without first
having been paid. If they
don't feel they can trust
their colleagues to pay for a
professional journal, why
should you think that you
can trust some stranger on
the opposite coast to pay
for your poetry mag?**

seriously enough. If you are in New York and a non-paying subscriber is in California, what can you do about it? Nothing. You can stop the subscription, but you can't collect for the issues that have already been sent.

If you seem to attract a high percentage of deadbeats, you should probably not accept sub-scriptions without payment enclosed. Or you can invoice for a new subscription, but not send the first issue — and certainly not the second — until you receive payment.

People do forget things, and libraries can be very slow. Plan on sending a second notice, but no more than that.

Samples

Charge for them. Most individuals — and even librarians — who request a sample will not subscribe after they receive it. There are people who try to get samples of everything they can and, with few ex-ceptions, are freeloaders who don't ever plan on buying. If anyone is seriously interested in subscribing to your magazine, then that person shouldn't hesitate to spend a mere 50¢ (or $1 or $2) for a sample copy.

Back Issues

What do you do with leftover copies? Save them. Large public libraries and university libraries, when they subscribe, will often want every issue from Number One on, even if you have been publishing for five years. Establish a back-issue price. Some little mags sell their back issues for the single copy rate; others, that have become somewhat successful, charge extremely high prices for their back issues. Let your conscience be your guide.

MISCELLANY

Advertising in the Magazine

Should you or should you not sell advertising? Probably not. To begin with, you cannot give an advertiser a good deal. Your circulation will be too small, your readership too limited, to make it worth his while. You've got to charge more than it is worth when you have a small-circulation periodical. If you charge only what it's worth, you are wasting your time.

Mass-circulation magazines derive their profits from their advertising. It's the only reason that their publishers are in business. For you, advertisers will be more of a bother. Unlike the big mags, they will not be the reason for your work, but an interruption of it. They have to be solicited and then catered to. They want to see proofs of the ad before it runs and, more often than not, they want to make changes. The few dollars that you can charge them isn't worth the trouble.

If you have good circulation among students in a high school or on a college campus, you might be able to sell advertising to local businesses, make some money on it, and still give the advertisers a good buy. You won't really *make* any money, but the income can help subsidize your printing costs. Your readers are the natural customers, under these circumstances, of pizza parlors, record shops and the like. (NOTE: Many newspapers demand cash with copy when they accept advertising from pizza shops. They do not wait until after the ad has been printed and then bill for it. You'd do well to follow the newspapers' example.)

One kind of advertising that many little mags do accept is *exchange advertising*. Some mags send out camera-ready copy to dozens of periodicals that they think might be sympathetic to their point of view. With the ad copy is a letter explaining that if you publish their ad they will publish one of a similar size in their magazine for you. This isn't a bad way to advertise. It doesn't cost either magazine anything but for the cost of preparing the ad. Whether you participate in exchange advertising or not depends on how much space you have to devote to that sort of thing.

Another kind of advertising popular with little mags and journals of opinion is classified advertising. Usually these are *un*classifieds. "Items for Sale" and "Apartments for Rent" are all mixed up together. Always get cash with copy when selling classifieds. An advertisement is such an ephemeral thing that the advertiser resents paying for it after it appears — especially if there are no takers for the items for sale.

If you do accept *display* advertising (large ads) you should establish a rate schedule: so much for a column-inch (one column wide x one inch deep), so much for an eighth-page, so much for a quarter-page, and so on. You might want to sell an extra color in an ad. Decide how much extra you must charge for that and set a minimum size for ads that are to have the color. You should also offer multiple insertion rates: the more times an ad runs unchanged, the less expensive per insertion. You must also specify if your rates apply to camera-ready copy or if you charge extra for composition.

Reviews

You know that books are reviewed, but did you know that periodicals are also reviewed? Well, they are. And a good review is the best selling tool you will ever have. There are thousands of periodicals published in the United States, and many more published around the world. How does a librarian sitting in the middle of

Indiana choose among them all? They come and go so quickly there's no way to keep up with them. Some magazines such as *National Geographic* and *Time* are so well established that they are standard library acquisitions. But what of relatively unknown journals such as yours? For guidance, librarians rely upon what the professional library journals have to say about them.

If your magazine is reviewed favorably by *Wilson Library Bulletin*, for example, you can quote that review in your advertising, and go on quoting it until the end of time. *"Highly recommended."—WILSON LIBRARY BULLETIN*. Never send out a mailing piece without that quote. It gives your magazine the often necessary credentials to be selected for a library's collection.

How will you know that you received a favorable review? Simple. The reviewing journal will send you a copy (along with a suggestion that you consider buying an ad). It might take months — even years — but if your magazine is any good, and if you survive, it will eventually be reviewed. The only way this will happen is if you send out copies of every issue to the reviewing journals. [See Appendix]

Microform Copies

Every year more and more libraries are deciding that they can no longer devote valuable shelf space to back issues of periodicals. To reduce the volume of printed matter that must be maintained, they are resorting to microfilm and microfiche storage.

A microfiche is a flat card containing a piece of film on which the pages of a periodical are reduced to a tiny size. This is inserted into a viewer and the person who wants to read the back issue can see it enlarged and projected on a rear-image screen. Microfilm accomplishes the same effect, but in reel form. It too projects on a rear-image screen or directly on a reading surface.

If you have many libraries as subscribers, you should make arrangements with one of the companies that offers microforms. Every year they will pay you a royalty on every copy they sold during the previous twelve months and they'll give you a free copy of the microform. They sell these only to subscribers to that particular magazine. In this way a non-subscriber is unable to buy just the microform and avoid paying the subscription money to the publisher. Along with the royalty check, the companies also provide a computer print-out of purchasers for comparison with subscription lists. It cost you nothing to offer this. Do it.

You can also make arrangements to have Xerox copies of back issues sold that you can no longer provide and for copies of individual articles bound into custom textbooks for classrooms. You'll get a royalty on these. [See Appendix]

Directories

Would-be subscribers may have seen or heard of your magazine, but not know your address. How do they find it? Librarians, and individuals who know about directories, will refer to *Ulrich's International Periodicals Directory* (in most any library) or to the *International Directory of Little Magazines and Small Presses* (in most large libraries). Listing is free and there's absolutely no excuse for your not being in these. [See Appendix]

The Reader's Guide to Periodical Literature

It is the dream of every little mag publisher to be included in the *Reader's Guide*. Being included there means that every subject, every author, and every article in every issue will be indexed and on record in every library in the United States. But it's a dream that rarely comes true.

The problem is the process by which indexed periodicals are selected. The subscribers vote on what periodicals are to be indexed. If you want to be included among those periodicals, you not only have to be on the shelves of a great many libraries (a thousand isn't nearly enough) but you also have to impress the librarians as worthy of being indexed.

Therefore, do not write to the *Reader's Guide* asking to be indexed. They can't help you.

Copyright

A copyright protects your magazine from unauthorized reproduction by someone else. There are some periodicals that welcome reprinting of material by whomever cares to do so. If this is the case with you, or if you just don't care, forget the copyright. If you'd like to have some control over what is reprinted, you should use a copyright.

There's been a big flap for years over the United States copyright laws. (Mark Twain was active in trying to get them changed.) In November of 1976 the first change since 1909 was finally enacted into law. It now protects printed material for the life of the author plus 50 years. This compares to a maximum of 56 years under the old law.

It also restricts the use of copying machines which had been outside the law in the past. An individual may now make a limited number of copies of copyrighted material, but not engage in systematic copying.

There are two ways to copyright material: 1, you can send $6 to the library of Congess, along with two copies of the magazine and a registration form, and then put the properly worded notice somewhere in the magazine or, 2, you can save $6 and just print the properly worded notice without the Library of Congress knowing anything about it. Both methods are perfectly legal and binding, but you must *register* and file a copy before instituting an infringement suit. The second method is recommended unless you have $6 to spare every time you publish an issue. [See Appendix]

If you don't want to bother with it at all, you should let your contributors know this so they can request that their articles or stories be copyrighted should they desire the protection.

Is It Worth It?

The odds of your being financially successful are somewhere in the range of one in five million, give or take a million, so let's not kid ourselves.

If you want to publish a magazine just for the pure joy or madness of it, for the sense of satisfaction you'll get from seeing a project through from the germ of an idea in your mind to the printed word on paper, then let nothing discourage you.

If you're in it for the money, forget it. On the other hand, Hugh Hefner pasted up the first issue of *Playboy* on his kitchen table . . .

Appendix
Glossary
Index

Appendix

ADDRESSING EQUIPMENT

Addresserette
Dymo Industries
Randolph Industrial Park
Randolph MA 02368

Addressograph
Addressograph-Multigraph
20602 Chagrin Blvd
Cleveland OH 44122

Mini-Master
South Shore Systems
P.O. Box 172
N. Abington MA 02351

Scriptomatic
Scriptomatic, Inc.
2030 Upland Way
Philadelphia PA 19131

ASSOCIATIONS

**CANADIAN PERIODICAL PUBLISHERS'
ASSOCIATION**
3 Church St.
Suite 407
Toronto, Ontario M5E 1M2
   The CPPA was organized to promote the cause
of periodicals owned and controlled by
Canadians. Membership is open to those
periodicals, large and small, that have had a
viable existence for at least 12 months and that
have been recommended for membership by two
current members.
   This is a very active organization that really
pushes to help its members increase their circulation with periodical displays, publication
and wide distribution of full-color catalogs, and
paid advertisements in the U.S. and Canada. A
monthly newsletter keeps members informed of
Arts Council grants, new review journals, etc.
   The membership fee is determined anew each
year (by the members), and low circulation mags
(under 2,000) are granted a reduction of 40%.

**COMMITTEE OF SMALL MAGAZINE EDITORS
AND PUBLISHERS**
P.O. Box 703
San Francisco CA 94101
Dues: $25 yearly
   In his book, *Democracy in America*, de
Tocqueville wrote, "In no country in the world

has the principle of association been more
successfully used, or more unsparingly applied
to a multitude of different objects, than in
America." Far be it from publishers of little mags
and small presses to stray from this tradition.
   COSMEP was founded in 1968 and has grown
to include 1200 members — only a fraction of the
total number of small presses in America, but a
fairly sizable group just the same. As with any
voluntary organization, the most aggressive
among the membership end up running it — but
this isn't to say that they can't be deposed at
election time. Any member is free to be
nominated to the governing body and to vote for
whomever he or she pleases.
   Why join at all? For one thing, you may be the
only person in your community publishing a little
mag. Joining puts you in touch with hundreds of
others like yourself who will share with you their
problems and their solutions. Beyond that, there
are very practical reasons for becoming a
member. COSMEP recently received a $30,000
grant to buy a truck which will be made into a
traveling bookstore to distribute small and
alternative press publications in areas where
they have not been available. Members can have
their titles or issues distributed in this way.
   Members also receive the COSMEP Newsletter
— a lively sheet that reflects the basically
anarchic character of the membership (everyone
is extremely independent) in addition to
publishing many items of interest about grants,
conferences, new periodicals, how-to articles,
etc.
   COSMEP also provides members with a
handbook on publishing (with sections on
distribution, library and bookstore sales,
promotion, production, printing and finances)
and with lists of libraries and bookstores on
labels at cheap rates.
   Joining is simple: there are no application
forms; you need only send in your dues and the
name and address of your press or periodical —
you can do this even if you haven't even
published anything yet.
   All in all, a good organization and worth
looking into.

BOOKS AND PERIODICALS

DIRECTORIES

ALTERNATIVES IN PRINT: catalog of social
change publications.
Glide Publications
330 Ellis St.
San Francisco CA 94102
198 pp. Paper; $8.95

This is the fifth edition of this growing directory. It began back in 1971 as the *Alternative Press Index* with only 200 publishers listed. In the 77-78 edition there are approximately 1,500 including producers of non-print media (records and films).

The directory is divided into four major sections: 1, a thesaurus of subjects form Abortion to Zionism with plenty of cross-indexing; 2, a subject index listing publishers under appropriate headings; 3, an alphabetized list of small presses and their publications; and 4, an address list of social change publishers arranged alphabetically by state.

If your publication is concerned with some aspect of social change, whether it be community control, ecology, gay liberation — whatever — let these people know about you. A lot of libraries subscribe and it would be to your advantage to be included.

One note, however: if you are *for* capital punishment and *against* the legalization of marijuana, *for* the right to carry a gun and *against* the Equal Rights Amendment, you can forget about being included. The editors do not consider anything that can not be even vaguely categorized as being on the "Left" as being an alternative. This is a pity because the book would be an even more valuable tool for librarians if it acknowledged the existence of the Right as well as the Left.

AYER DIRECTORY OF PUBLICATIONS
Ayer Press
W. Washington Square
Philadelphia PA 19063

Both magazines and newspapers are included here. The periodicals are listed alphabetically — first by states, then by cities within the states, and then by titles. If you sell advertising, you should be in here. No charge for listing.

BOWKER BOOK DIRECTORIES
R. R. Bowker Co.
1180 Avenue of the Americas
New York NY 10036

American Book Trade Directory
Books in Print
Bowker's Medical Books in Print
Children's Book in Print
Elementary High School Books in Print
Paperbound Books in Print
Subject Guide to Children's Books in Print
Subject Guide to Books in Print

Write to Bowker asking for information on any of the directories that interest you.

BRITISH DIRECTORY OF LITTLE MAGAZINES AND SMALL PRESSES
Headland Publications
56, Blakes Lane
New Malden, Surrey, England KT3 6NX
Paper; $1.00

All the U.K. entries culled from the *International Directory* and bound into one volume.

CENSORED
762 Avenue "N" S.E.
Winter Haven FL 33880
24 pp; $3.00

Most directories of little mags and small presses can generally be described as "left-wing" whether they agree with that designation or not. But this is one directory of "right-wing" periodicals. They are listed in alphabetical order under various categories (newsletters, magazines, etc.). Opposite each listing is a descriptive comment such as this (for *American Opinion* published by the John Birch Society): "Thoughtful, readable, in-depth articles on backgrounds of social, economic and political affairs."

Also listed are book publishers, organizations, and sympathetic distributors.

A DIRECTORY OF AMERICAN FICTION WRITERS
Paper, $6.00; cloth, $12.00.
132 pages.

A DIRECTORY OF AMERICAN POETS
Paper, $5.00; cloth, $10.00.
136 pages.

Poets & Writers, Inc.
201 West 54th St.
New York NY 10019

These directories provide a comprehensive compilation of poets and fiction writers publishing in the United States today. (1,500 poets; 800 writers.) All poets and fiction writers who have published in book form or whose work has appeared recurrently in nationally published periodicals are eligible to apply for listing.

The primary purpose of the directories is to assist in locating these writers for readings, workshops, and other assignments. They are also useful reference works for libraries with contemporary poetry collections, and they have helped innumerable book and magazine publishers reach contemporary authors.

Author entries are organized geographically by state of primary residence, and listed alphabetically within each state grouping. The *Directory of American Poets* has an index of authors with specific ethnic backgrounds (Black, Native American, etc.). For each author, the directories provide current address, telephone number, work preference, linguistic abilities, and most recent book.

In addition to author listings, the *Directory of American Fiction Writers* also lists 500 organizations that sponsor readings and workshops, listings of anthologies, films, and videotapes of contemporary authors, resources for creative writing teachers, information about literary organizations and publications useful to writers, bookstores that stock poetry, fine fiction, and literary magazines, and a practical checklist to guide organizers of readings and workshops.

A single supplement updates and augments both directories and is mailed free to purchasers.

If you buy either of the directories in a bookstore, a postcard is enclosed to notify Poets & Writers that you are eligible to receive the Supplement.

Because writers and poets are at least as mobile as any other category, the directories are out-of-date on the day they are published. No problem. If a letter to an author comes back marked "Moved — No Forwarding Address," simply call (212) 757-1766 COLLECT (!) and you'll be given the latest information available. For that matter, they invite you to call them collect if you have any questions about any of the information in the directories. (This service was made possible through support from the Literature Program of the National Endowment for the Arts.)

DIRECTORY OF LOCAL POETRY GROUPS
Workshop Press Ltd.
2 Culham Court
Granville Road
London, N.4, England
Paper; 50p

A comprehensive directory of British poetry groups and associations.

DIRECTORY OF SMALL MAGAZINE/PRESS EDITORS AND PUBLISHERS
Dustbooks
P.O. Box 1056
Paradise CA 95969
156 pages; $4.95

This is an annual publication giving the names of editors and publishers arranged alphabetically (3,000 or so names in the 7th edition and growing every year). Each listing also gives the name of the press or magazine (and its address) with which the individual is associated. If there are co-editors/publishers, their names are cross-referenced.

In earlier editions when there were only half as many names listed, the editors were given the opportunity to say something about themselves: their personal reading preferences, influences, and reasons for editing and publishing. This made for interesting browsing* and was very helpful to writers when trying to decide whether or not a particular story or poem might have appeal to a particular editor. Dustbooks must have felt that it was getting unwieldly. The names and addresses are now simply extracted *International Directory of Little Magazines and Small Presses.*

*For a sample, see "Why Do They Do It?" on pages 4 and 5 of this book.

DIRECTORY OF WOMEN'S MEDIA
3306 Ross Place, N.W.
Washington D.C. 20008
$8.00

A directory of women's periodicals, presses, media courses, film, video. radio TV, art/graphics/theatre, music, media organizations, speakers bureaus, library collections, selected directories and catalogs, bookstores, news services, columns, distributors, multi-media and individual media women.

SMALL PRESS RECORD OF BOOKS
Dustbooks
P.O. Box 1056
Paradise CA 95969
208 pages; paper, $6.95

4,000 or so books, pamphlets, chapbooks, broadsides, posters, and poem-cards published by nearly 1,000 small presses. Very few of these works have found their way into *Books in Print*.

Each entry is indexed three ways: by author, by title, by publisher. Arrangements are alphabetical in all cases, with cross-referencing where there is more than one author (or editor) of a given work. A complete listing in the author index contains author/editor's name, title of work, publisher's name, dimensions, number of pages, type of binding and printing, price, publication date, and comment or description. A few typical examples:

Helick, R. Martin, *ELEMENTS OF PRESCHOOL PLAYYARDS*, Regent Graphic Services. 12x9; cl/$15.00; 1973, 1974. Idea-source for the design of preschool playyards.

Schraeger, Samuel P. Jr., *COULD NOT KEEP FROM GOING SIDEWAYS*, Realities. 6x9; 32pp; lo; pa/$2.00; 1975. Collection of poetry and short stories by author.

Tulku, Tharthang, ed., *TIBETAN THANKA PORTFOLIO*, Charma. 11x8½; 20pp; lo; cl/$25.00; 1975. 20 full-color reproductions of Tibetan paintings with descriptions.

If you have something that you would like listed (no periodicals), write to Dustbooks requesting a form.

ULRICH'S INTERNATIONAL PERIODICALS DIRECTORY
R. R. Bowker
1180 Avenue of the Americas
New York NY 10036

A standard acquisition for most libraries. There's no excuse for not being listed here. Do it. It's free.

WRITER'S DIGEST MARKET GUIDES
9933 Alliance Road
Cincinnati OH 45242

Arts & Crafts Market
800 pp; cloth; $10.95

Photographer's Market
400 pp; cloth; $9.95

Writer's Market
1,000 pp; cloth; $13.95

The *Writer's market* is already a standard library acquisistion and the other two (*Arts & Crafts*, 4th edition; *Photographer's*, new this year) will probably become so also. Altogether, the 1978 directories list over 10,000 markets (with lots of duplicates among the three of course) for freelance writers, artists, cartoonists, designers, photographers, calligraphers, animators, poets, essayists — whoever.

The question is, do you want *your* press listed in any of these? Maybe they don't want you.

Although more and more space is being devoted each year to small and independent presses, there's a limit to how many pages they can bind into *Writer's Market*, for example, and still be able to charge a reasonable price for it.

What does inclusion mean to you? Probably that you will get many more unsolicited submissions than you would otherwise, and this means that you will get many more unusable pieces that you will have to send back. On the other hand, you might get some gems that somebody else would have gotten instead.

Each publisher that is included is allowed a paragraph or so to describe current needs. With these directories, as with anywhere else you invite submissions, keep the description of what you are looking for as narrow as possible. If it's too general, you'll be flooded with material that has no relevance to what you are trying to publish (and you'll get plenty of that anyway).

In addition to listings of markets, the books have many articles on how to sell material, how to keep records, copyright laws, etc. These books are a must for writers, artists, and photographers who haven't agents out peddling their stuff for them.

EDITING

CODA: Poets & writers newsletter
201 West 54 St.
New York NY 10019
5 issues; $6.00 year.

Although it says "poets & writers" in the subtitle, editors and publishers of little mags and small presses will find this newsletter quite valuable. (Most of them think of themselves as poets or writers anyway.)

There's lots of hard information here. The June/July 1977 issue, for example, has as its lead article an excellent analysis of the book club business, followed by a short piece on the economics of reprinting "lost American fiction", (the many good, well-received novels that go out of print and simply become forgotten).

Other topics that *Coda* reports on include: writer's colonies, taxes and the writer, publishing activities and opportunities, copyright protection, book distribution, grants and awards, book fairs and festivals, writers available for readings and workshops, services for writers, editors, publishers, etc.

Each issue is 32-36 pages. This is a good buy.

EDITING THE SMALL MAGAZINE
By Rowena Ferguson
Columbia University Press
562 West 113th St.
New York NY 10025
Revised Edition; 221 pages; cloth, $10.00; paper, $3.95.

When using the term "small magazines," Ms. Ferguson is referring to a somewhat different category than is usually meant by "*little* magazines."

She defines a small magazine as the child of a parent body (a club or organization of some kind) which is not of itself in the publishing business.

The small magazine carries little or no advertising and, in any case, does not rely upon this revenue. Its continued existence depends instead upon a subsidy obtained either by membership dues or through a budget appropriation. And, last, its circulation is limited and often controlled.

The advice that she gives — and it is all good advice — is not intended as much for the free-wheeling editor as it is for the "captive" editor: that man or woman who has been assigned, and may even be paid, to publish a specific kind of periodical for a specific audience. Such an audience might be composed of employees of a large corporation or the members of a social, religious or professional organization.

Because Ms. Ferguson has had a great deal of experience as an editor of a wide range of publications, she is able to give practical pointers on basic editorial policy, editorial planning, the procuring and processing of manuscripts, and layout and design.

All in all, a good book for anyone who has the responsibility of editing a house organ or organization newsletter.

LIFELINE: a meeting place for writers, poets, illustrators and publishers
Highway Book Shop
300,000 Yonge St.
Cobalt, Ontario
POJ 1CO
24 issues yearly; $15.00

Cobalt, Ontario once was—and perhaps still is—the center of a rich silver-mining district. Douglas Pollard, editor and publisher of *Lifeline* has now made Cobalt the site of a goldmine. It's a rare issue that doesn't yield a nugget or two for any of the potential subscribers listed in the newsletter's subtitle.

For no charge at all, publishers can list their needs, and writers their completed manuscripts. In addition, there are always two or three pages of paid classifieds and listings of freelance artists, editors, and writers.

If you're hesitant to lay out $15, you can send just $2 for three consecutive issues.

THE LITTLE MAGAZINE AND CONTEMPORARY LITERATURE
Modern Language Association
60 Fifth Avenue
New York NY 10011
119 pages; paper;$1.25

This is the transcript of a symposium held in the spring of 1965 at the Library of Congress and sponsored by the Carnegie Corporation. It was a stellar assemblage of little mag personalities: George Plimpton of *Partisan Review*, Karl Shapiro formerly of *Poetry* and *Praire Schooner*, Theodore Weiss of the *Quarterly Review of Literature*, Jules Chametzky of the *Massachusetts Review*, Reed Whitmore of the *Carleton Miscellany*, along with representatives of some 50 other journals. Even Alan Tate, one of the original Fugitives, and Alan Swallow (who unfortunately died the following year) were there.

It is an odd thing to read this collection of speeches and remarks by mainly academic types with their talk of foundation grants and university censorship — and innumerable obscure quotations.

During the open discussion portions of the symposium, many people got up to speak little pieces that had nothing to do with what had transpired immediately before. One got the feeling that this was because they were not listening to what went before, but were composing their little pieces.

At one point, Louis Rubin and Thomas Parkins became involved in a professorial display of erudition regarding the relative placement of values in *Middlemarch* and *Another Country*. There was a lot of this sort of discussion. Nearly the entire symposium itself would have been "another country" to the publishers of most contemporary little mags. In fact, there was just one speaker with whom they could readily identify, and that was George Hitchcock of *Kayak* (which he is still publishing):

"I feel out of place . . . You guys have all been talking as if you were tired salesmen and boondogglers. My own feeling about editing is if you don't get any joy out of it, if you don't feel it, if your blood doesn't flow when you do it, then get the hell out of it . . . In my own case I simplify the problem (of finance and distribution) as much as I can by not printing more than five hundred copies and by printing them all myself . . . It's a basement enterprise. And I feel anyone who wants to edit a little magazine enough can do that."

One must remember that the symposium was held the very year when the first edition of the *International Directory* was published (with only 250 listings compared to 2,000 in the latest). Probably three-fourths of all little mags were still being published by expensive letterpress (one of the contributing factors to — or, at least, one of the excuses for — the demise of the *Kenyon Review*). Things *were* different just a dozen years ago. Few people had Hitchcock's printing expertise. Nowadays, anyone with a felt-tip pen and $20 for a quicky printer can publish a poetry journal.

It will take you only a couple of hours to read the proceedings of this two-day meeting for which the Carnagie Corporation spent thousands to transport the participants to Washington, feed them, and house them. If —but only if — you are a student of little mags, it's worth a buck and a quarter.

MODERN MAGAZINE EDITING

By Robert Root
William C. Brown Co.
2460 Kerper Blve.
Dubuque IA 52001
558 pages; cloth, $9.95.

The revolution in printing technology has accelerated to the point where the latest piece of equipment is out-of-date on the day it is installed. So a book written in 1965-66 with chapters on the subject of magazine production can hardly be called "modern" in 1977-78 — and beyond. Maybe the book will be revised before its next printing.

In spite of the fact that the book doesn't even acknowledge the existence of computer typesetting, transfer lettering, or many of the other standard tools of the present-day magazine editor and publisher, there are sections still relevant to anyone who wishes to pursue the art.

Root planned it as a textbook specifically for a course in basic magazine editing, and if used as a *supplementary* text rather than as *the* text (as it was intended) it can still be useful. Chapters on "The Editor's Job," "Copyediting," "The Editor and Literary Style," and the like all contain good medicine for would-be (and many practicing) editors.

GRAPHIC ARTS

ART AND REPRODUCTION: Graphic *reproduction techniques*
By Raymond A. Ballinger
Van Nostrand Reinhold
450 West 33rd St.
New York NY 10001
112 pages; paper, $7.95; cloth, $12.95.

Ballinger is concerned with the materials and techniques available to the modern graphic artist — without really showing how to use them. He gives examples galore, but precious few directions about how to get there from here. In his introduction he admits that this "is not a how-to-do-it publication." It is intended, he asserts, to be "an inspirational book to help young designers to be *total* designers through their interest in design, preparatory, and reproduction processes and in the contemporary materials at their command." Oh, maybe.

The contents page looks as though the book could fulfill this promise (Halftones, Four-color Printing, Binding, etc.) but what appears on the pages is usually a quick look at some bare bones already quite familiar to designers of even limited experience, without any real meat for the inexperienced who wants to know more.

The book has been compiled and pasted-up rather than designed and written. Any inspiration offered can be gotten much more cheaply by requesting brochures and samples from paper manufacturers — the book falls into that category.

BASIC PHOTOGRAPHY FOR THE GRAPHIC ARTS
Kodak Publication Q-1
Eastman Kodak Company
Rochester NY 14650
48 pages; paper, $3.00

Here are the basics (and some fine points) explained with clear instructions and plenty of illustrations: line, continuous-tone, and halftone images; equipment needed by the process camera operator; how to shoot and process film; the use of the gray scale; an explanation of PMT's; stripping in negs; platemaking; plus much more.

All in all, a good introduction for the beginner.

DESIGNING . . . FOR MAGAZINES
By Jan V. White
R. R. Bowker
1180 Avenue of the Americas
New York NY 10036
176 pages; cloth, $16.95

Jan White's concern is with the effective display of graphic elements in aesthetically pleasing designs. To illustrate his points he uses many before and after reproductions from actual magazines that he has helped redesign. So many, in fact, that the book could have been titled, "Famous Magazines That Have Known Me." He might have been even more instructive had he selected from among other popular journals and discussed their graphic transformations.

But all this is beside the point. His designs are readable, attractive, interesting, and very 1970's in appearance. Ten-fifteen years from now the book will look dated, but that doesn't detract from its usefulness now. (Anyway, if someone knew what type faces were going to be in vogue in 1990, he'd be using his crystal ball to win horse races and to buy stock.)

Probably the book's greatest value is that it shows how to go about designing good-looking covers and pages on a limited budget. Mr.White goes in heavily for rules and borders, crisp typography, and the effective use of white space — graphic elements available to even the most impecunious of editors. He designed the book itself along these lines, and a very inviting book it is. There are seven sections: Covers, Contents, Flash Forms, Departments, Editorials, Openers, and Products, each composed of clearly written explanatory text and many illustrative examples.

Except for cover and page reproductions, and dummy pages of solutions to various layout problems, the only other illustrations he uses are out-of-copyright engravings. (Even though White takes credit for "unearthing" them himself, one suspects — one would be willing to bet — that they came from Dover's *Picture Sourcebook for Collage and Decoupage*, and from the Dover edition of Gustave Dore's Bible.) He selected these *because* of their "totally unsuitable character, which can be the basis for humor; as well as for their colorfulness." They add a lot to a book that would have been much drier without them — and there's a lesson here, too.

The $16.95 price might be a little much for a beginning publisher, but all college libraries, high schools with graphic arts programs, and main public libraries should own this book.

EXPLORING THE WORLD OF GRAPHIC COMMUNICATIONS
Graphics Markets Division
Eastman Kodak Company
Rochester NY 14650

Book 1, Basic Printing Methods
Kodak Publication No. GA-11-1
28 pages; $2.00

Book 2, Graphic Design
Kodak Publication No. GA-11-2
40 pages; $6.50

These are the first two of a projected 10-volume series of pamphlets on the graphic arts. They are intended for student use in conjunction with classroom instruction, but would serve the purpose of presenting basics to anyone wanting this information.

As you might guess, they are very slickly done: lots of illustrations (many in full color) and good clear text. The prices seem a little high ($6.50 for a 40-page pamphlet?), but there must certainly be bulk rates for classroom use.

Basic Printing Methods clearly explains the differences among the various methods — offset, gravure, screen printing, and letterpress — and has short discussions on inks and papers.

Graphic Design covers design techniques (screen tints, special effects with photographs, etc.), color theory, type styles, and an excellent chapter on graphic arts measurements (word spacing, line spacing, and copyfitting).

Future books in the series will be: 3, Creative Photography; 4, Copy Preparation; 5, Photoreproduction; 6, Film Assembly and Offset Platemaking; 7, Offset Presswork; 8, Finishing; 9, Student Activity Guide; and 10, Instructor's Guide.

FINE PRINT: A review for the arts of the book.
P.O. Box 7741
San Francisco CA 94120
Quarterly; $10 year

If you want to publish a book or magazine but you're turned off, on the one hand, by square bindings and typewriter type, and on the other, by computer-produced, glued-together commercial books, then you're probably a spiritual brother or sister of *Fine Print* subscribers, and you might consider becoming a subscriber yourself.

The editors are dedicated to the art of producing and collecting fine limited edition books. They feature articles on typography, calligraphy, hand bookbinding, papermaking, book illustration, and profiles of prominent presses and people in the field. (What other journal, in its reviews, would tell you who made the *paper* the books reviewed were printed on?) Also included are reviews of new small press books and books about bookmaking along with a calender of exhibits and events around the USA and abroad.

The magazine itself is a tribute to fine printing, and each issue is designed by a different prominent typographer-printer.

GRAPHIC ARTS
By Darvery E. Carlsen
Chas. A. Bennett Co., Inc.
809 W. Detweiller Dr.
Peoria IL 61614
208 pages; cloth, $6.00

This is a textbook intended for high school classes and, as such, is eminently suitable for the task (especially when accompanied by a competent instructor). Plenty of clear step-by-step text with two to four pictures on every page to make the text even clearer.

For an amateur who's picked up an old platen press or offset press (and no instruction booklet to go with it) this book would be well worth the price.

Often, publishers of little mags can do more interesting customizing with their journals than the giants can because they have only 100 or 200 copies to print. For example, suppose you decided to have a thermograved (raised printing) cover: this book shows you how to do it. Suppose you wanted to silk screen the cover, or to bind in a block print: again, this book shows you how. It even tells you how to make your own paper.

Carlsen explains bookbinding, photography, mimeograph machines, spirit duplicators, and photo-copying. A reasonably intelligent person can, at the least, get the basics from this book, and then go on to bigger and better things. There's not much on preparing camera-ready art since the book is really intended more for production people than artists, but if you want to get into printing, here's a good place to start.

One thing it will do: it will teach you the printer's vocabulary so that you needn't sound like a ninny when you go in to talk to him.

KODAK HANDBOOK OF NEWSPAPER TECHNIQUES
Kodak Graphic Arts Data Book No. Q-165H
Eastman Kodak Company
Rochester NY 14650
40 pages; cloth, $6.95

The publisher of the *Hometown Daily Blatt* and the *Southside Underground Rag* are both faced with similar obstacles in the production of their respective — if not always respected — newspapers: ulcer-causing deadlines, late-breaking stories, nit-picking advertisers, last-minute changes, and the need to fill every column-inch with *something*.

This book shows the techniques used to overcome those obstacles — from composition to color separation. Although newspapers have many printing techniques in common with other printing trades, the flow of work is somewhat different than, say, a job shop, and it would pay anyone who is contemplating publishing an independent newspaper to study this introduction to newspaper techniques.

MORE SPECIAL EFFECTS FOR REPRODUCTION
Kodak Publication Q-171
Eastman Kodak Company
Rochester NY 14650
80 pages; paper, $12.00

The process camera operator as graphic artist. Tips with some truly inspiring examples of photo modification for special effects: posterizing, duotones, tone-line process, line posterization, and the very sophisticated scanner effects (which involve lasar beams and computers among other things).

For most of the varieties of the different techniques described there are complete, step-by-step instructions. And for every illustration printed there are complete production data.

This is high-class work and was produced using the best of equipment. But even without access to a Saltzman diffusion enlarger with Super Chromega F dichroic head or a Klimsch Super Autovertika "60" camera or 3000-watt Ascorlux pulsed-xenon arc lamps, one can still produce dramatic and even startling effects in the darkroom using this book as a general guide.

MAKE YOUR OWN COMICS FOR FUN AND PROFIT
By Richard Cummings
David McKay Company
750 Third Ave.
New York NY 10017
118 pages; cloth, $8.95

Many writers and editors also have artistic ability. They can take advantage of this talent in their publishing enterprises.

Richard Cummings, with the help of such famous cartoonists as Richard Corben (who produced many well-known underground cartoons), Marie Severin (*MAD*), and Jules Feiffer (whom everybody knows), along with many unknown younger cartoonists, guides you through the processes necessary to produce your own cartoons.

The book is divided into five sections: Ideas, Style, Story, Rendering, and Publication. There's as much inspiration here as there is how-to.

PUBLICATION DESIGN: *A guide to page layout, typography, format and style*
By Allen Hulburt
Van Nostrand Reinhold
450 West 33rd St.
New York NY 10001
134 pages; paper, $7.95; cloth, $12.95

Many periodicals are quite prosaic. Some publishers keep them that way intentionally, either because they want to save their fireworks for within the actual printed words, or because they think that a little graphic modishness will detract from the dignity of their high-falutin' journal. But is there any reason why *any* magazine should be drab and forbidding? A scholarly journal need not have bright splashes of color or far-out super-graphics, but even formality deserves thoughtful design. Then there are those publishers who stick to the commonplace only because of timidity. They don't know anything else, and they are afraid to *try* anything else.

A stroll through Hurlburt's excellent book will show all these people that type and paper are not merely the necessaries for permitting a reader to absorb another's words, but can, in themselves, convey meaning, and that there is a relationship between the words and their presentation.

Hurlburt traces the historical development of the modern magazine from it's beginnings in the 1920's with the typographic experiments of the Bauhaus designers and their influence on such magazines as *Vanity Fair, Fortune,* and *Harper's Bazaar,* and on through the *Rolling Stone/Playboy* age of today. He shows why it is important for the page designer to study and understand the principles of design (such as in the Japanese tatami mat and Le Corbusier's modular system) so that he can give a coherence to his pages in a world cluttered with confusing images. Photographs and artwork are no longer incidental to the printed word, but are themselves sources of information both factual and metaphoric.

The book is divided into two sections: the first (the contents of which are merely suggested above) is concerned with the art "spirit," and the second with craft and techniques. In the second section Hurlburt discusses color, the grid approach to page design, typography, and layout and design.

He offers, pretty much, that which he suggests in his introduction the publication designer needs to understand: ". . . the current lines and techniques of visual communication and the basic principles that have guided other designers. In addition, he will benefit from an awareness of the forces outside the design fraternity that contributes to the success or failure of his efforts."

STUDIO TIPS FOR ARTISTS & GRAPHIC DESIGNERS
By Bill Gray
Van Nostrand Reinhold
450 West 33rd St.
New York NY 10001
128 pages; paper; $4.95

There are little tricks and techniques that most graphic artists learn sooner or later. But why wait until later? With Bill Gray's book you can learn them now.

Many of these tips are not even taught in art schools. Normally, one learns them on-the-job through inspired problem-solving, or from an older artist with whom one works. Bill Gray is an old artist (50 years on the job) and he knows *all* the tricks.

He tells you how to keep ink bottles from tipping over, how to revive neglected brushes, how to flatten curled prints, how to clean up spilled rubber cement, how to prevent stacked pieces of poster board from sliding, and many other studio maintenance tips.

He also has many production tips: how to make a 3-D design photographically, how to make a film-strip of your own original alphabet, how to make watercolors stick to shiny surfaces, how to draw ovals, how to make templates for repeating patterns, etc.

Altogether there are 145 well-written tips (hand-lettered in legible italics, in fact), and each is clearly illustrated, usually one tip to a page. This is a got-to-have book for the neophyte, and an ought-to-have book for the experienced. Nearly any one of the tips is worth the purchase price. Don't wait until you've been on the job 50 years to learn all this.

U&lc: *Upper &Lower Case, the international journal of typographics*
216 East 45 St.
New York NY 10017
Quarterly; Free.

To begin with, not just anybody can receive this magazine. Because it is free, the publishers have to determine that those receiving it will be of some value to those who advertise within its pages (and it is they, after all , who pay the price of all those free subscriptions). If you can convince them that you are in fact a bona fide and regular user of *type* — and not just a typesetter, or buyer of someone else's type, but a frequent user of typography in a creative manner — then they will put you on their mailing list.

You can often judge a periodical's readership as much by its advertisements as by its editorial matter. *U&lc* has ads placed by phototypositer manufacturers, transfer letter manufacturers, typographers, and the like. The editorial matter ranges quite far, from cartoons to photographs to 19th-century posters, but never out of sight of shore where stands a happy crowd of imaginative graphic designers. The physical magazine itself is a laboratory of typographical experiments.

If you can convince these people that you should be receiving their periodical, they will reward your persistence.

PHOTOGRAPHY

KODAK BOOKS AND PAMPHLETS
Eastman Kodak Company
Department 454
343 State St.
Rochester NY 14650

The Eastman Kodak Company publishes a huge library of books and pamphlets on just about everything related to photography — amateur, professional, and technical — from a *Multilingual Glossary of Motion Picture Terms* to instructions on how to take photographs through a miscroscope. Those listed below are just a few that will be of interest to the editor/publisher of a little magazine or small press.

There was a time when all of Kodak's smaller pamphlets were punched with 17 square holes, and if you wanted to keep them in a binder, you had to buy a special 17-prong binder available only from Kodak. For reasons known best to their Binder Sales Manager, Kodak now punches the pamphlets with *six round* holes. Too bad if you bought a 17-pronger — it is now inoperative and you must buy a special 6-prong binder (at $3.25 and it's designed to hold only 6 pamphlets).

Advanced Camera Techniques For 126 and 35mm Cameras
Code Number AC-56
52 pages; $1.95
Short discussions of lenses, camera handling, action pictures, exposure meters, flash photography, close-ups, etc.

Adventures in Existing-Light Photography
Code Number AC-44
64 pages; $1.50
You can't always have a flash available — and for many pictures you don't want one. Here are many suggestions for using existing light, both to get a good picture and for special effects. The pamphlet includes an excellent chart of suggested exposures for Kodak films under a variety of conditions, e.g. candlelight, fireworks, night football.

Basic Developing, Printing, Enlarging in Black-and-White
Code Number AJ-2
72 pages; $1.75
Step-by-step instructions with pictures showing the basic equipment needed and the processes to be followed to turn your exposed (but as yet undeveloped) black-and-white film into finished photographs. This is a good first-book for anyone getting into darkroom techniques.

Filters and Lens Attachments for Black-and-White and Color Pictures
Code Number AB-1
72 pages; $1.95

You can produce some startling effects — and sometimes just make better pictures — by using the proper filters. Many amateur photographers never bother with filters, but they can be a lot of fun. While most of this pamphlet is concerned with color photography, there are some good hints for black-and-white.

How to Make Good Pictures
Code Number AW-1
192 pages; $2.95
As pointed out in the book's introduction, this isn't a technical book. For the most part it simply points out some of the features that make pictures better than run-of-the-mill, and suggests ideas for shooting good pictures with the least possible fuss and expense. Basically for the Instamatic owner, it's still a good book for anyone who doesn't already consider himself a professional.

Student Pictures for School Publications
Code Number AT-13
16 pages; 20c
A collection of photo ideas for the student journalist.

Photolab Design
Code Number K-13
$2.00
This pamphlet used to be called *Darkroom Design and Construction* and sold for 50¢. When the price went up to $1 they glorified the darkroom and called it a photolab. Now it's $2, but they must not have been able to think up an even fancier name. Actually, it's a pretty good look at what's required in a professional darkroom and worth the two bucks if you're planning on spending a few grand building or remodeling.

Index to Kodak Information
Code Number L-5
44 pages; Free
Over 850 pamphlets, books, dataguides, and specialty items are listed here ranging in price from 5¢ to $15.95 (and a few freebies). The more you know, the more you'll want to know, and you're bound to find some technical literature here that you'll want to add to your graphic arts library.

PUBLISHING

FOLIO: *The magazine for magazine management*
125 Elm St., P.O. Box 697
New Canaan CT 06840
Monthly [6 full issues, 6 update news editions]
$22 year
This is a slick journal intended for professionals — and is better than most trade journals in other fields.

Lots of practical articles written by publishing, marketing, and management consultants. Topics range from "Saving money on your composition" to "What the new copyright law means to you."

A new feature that began with the April 1977 issue is "Graphic idea notebook." It is intended to be a regular series of swipe file pages to act as thought-provoking idea starters put together from an editor's point of view. The first was a six-page collection of various ways to use numerals; the second, a seven-page collection of graphically interesting ways to employ maps.

Just as useful to the beginning publisher are the advertisements. There are many services, supplies, and pieces of equipment that every commercial publisher ought to know about. The ads will provide an acquaintance with them.

HOW TO PUBLISH, PROMOTE AND SELL YOUR BOOK: *A guide for the self-publishing author*
By Joseph V. Goodman
Adams Press
30 W. Washington St.
Chicago IL 60602
65 pages; paper, $3

Here is a down-to-earth how-to book for the aspiring author who cannot find a commercial publisher willing to publish his or her *magnum opus*. Goodman begins with the premise that if no commercial publisher will touch the manuscript, then it almost certainly will not be a commercial success no matter how well it is written — and chances are, it's not very good anyway. But if you're determined to go through with it, he tells you what you must do.

Goodman has a lot of practical advice (even reminding authors to arrange for a place to store all those cartons of books when they arrive), he lists plenty of helpful addresses (review journals, wholesale distributors, etc.), includes lots of miscellaneous tips (most writers misspell "Foreword"), and closes with a sound indictment of the vanity press.

If your Great American Novel has been turned down by publisher after publisher, but you feel that it's your duty to make sure that the public is not deprived of its wonders, then you should spend $3 for this little book. It could be worth much more than that to you.

HOW TO PUBLISH YOUR OWN BOOK: A Guide *for authors who wish to publish a book at their own expense.*
By L. W. Mueller
Harlo Press
16721 Hamilton Ave.
Detroit MI 48203
180 pages; $6.95 hardbound, $4.95 softbound.

It's a short step from magazine publishing to book publishing, and many, many small presses produce both. While there are any number of similarities between the two enterprises, there are enough differences to make a separate book on the subject well worth the reading.

A commercial book publisher must sell 6,000 or more copies of a book in order to make a profit. This is why only a tiny few of the uncountable manuscripts that are submitted unsolicited are ever accepted. A college student may have spent an extremely interesting semester in a foreign university, but there couldn't conceivably be 6,000 people who would want to read, *My Sojurn in Taiwan: a student's recollections of college life in the Orient.* If that student is absolutely determined to get his book into print, there are only two choices: he can publish it himself, or he can pay a "vanity" publisher to print it for him.

Mueller, after 30 years in the printing and publishing business, recommends that he print it himself. In fact, he comes down quite hard on the vanity presses or, as they prefer to call themselves, "subsidy publishers." He points out that they do not generate any sales and that the costs of using them are too high. He sums up the general feeling of those who have gone the vanity press route: "If I'm going to do practically all of the work, why spend so much money, and why not receive the full amount of the sales, rather than the 'forty percent royalty' vanity publishers refer to?"

With this in mind, Mueller tells how to do it yourself: Among other things, he offers advice about manuscript preparation, selecting a book printer, determining the number of copies to print, proofreading and choosing the kind of paper and binding.

An especially interesting feature is a 24-page section which shows examples of the typical processes for reproducing illustrations (line drawings, halftones, duotones, and four-color), and the effect different papers have on reproductive quality.

He also discusses Library of Congress Catalog Card Numbers and International Standard Book Numbers.

Once a book is produced, the major problem the self-publishing author (as well as the large publisher) faces, is selling it. Mueller has chapters on promoting a book before and after publication, and techniques for selling by direct mail, space advertising, and through normal channels: bookstores, libraries, jobbers, etc. He even shows how to prepare invoices.

Glossary and bibliography.

HOW TO START A HIGH SCHOOL UNDERGROUND PAPER
Youth Liberation
2007 Washtenaw Ave.
Ann Arbor MI 48104
Revised edition; 48 pages; 50¢

There was a time, not all that long ago, when no high school student would dare to publish and then sell on school property any periodical that was not authorized by the administration and produced with the "guidance" of a faculty advisor. There are still such periodicals, but there are now also scores of "underground" papers being published independently.

For the past few years, Youth Liberation has been encouraging this activity. One of the organization's projects has been the distribution of this how-to pamphlet. Over 10,000 copies of the first version have been sold since 1970. A much enlarged and more professionally produced edition will be available in early 1978.

In addition to the technical aspects of publishing, the pamphlet includes a lively history of the high school underground press (drawn from YL's archives of over 500 different papers), in-depth studies of two of the papers, information about political hassles, First Amendment freedoms, and other problems that student publishers (and adults, too, for that matter) ought to know.

HOW TO PUBLISH YOUR OWN BOOK. SONG. COURSE. SLIDE CHART. OR OTHER PRINTED PRODUCT. & MAKE IT GO !
By Duane Shinn
Shinn Music Aids
5090 Dobret
Central Point OR 97501
118 Pages; loose-leaf, $19.95.

We've all seen advertisements for seminars that, it is claimed, will make us more successful in life. Duane Shinn attended one in 1965 and, by golly, became successful. Whether or not this really had anything to do with the seminar, we'll never know — but *he* thinks it did. In this loose-leaf binder filled with tips and encouragement, he shares with us some of what he learned in that seminar and a lot of what he has learned since.

Actually, it's a good collection of nuts and bolts information about how to manufacture and sell printed material — along with just enough evangelicalism to spur would-be entrepreneurs.

Many publishers of little mags, once having discovered the secrets of printing, branch out into related areas. They publish directories chapbooks, how-to-do-its, newsletters, etc. Shinn tells them how to come up with new ideas, how to test them, and how to market them. He has been successful in publishing a dozen or more items ranging from a strum-along guitar chart to a pamphlet entitled, "How to Redecorate Your Old Piano. . . And Make It Look Great!" In addition to the text (printed on un-numbered pages) he has included samples of his products and a variety of merchandising gimmicks.

If your goal is to become a successful, if moderately small, independent businessperson, you ought to consider buying this.

THE HUENEFELD REPORT: *For managers and planners in modest-sized book publishing houses.*

P.O. Box U
Bedford MA 01730
Bi-weekly
$38 year.

If you think it's difficult to self-publish a book, just wait until you try to sell all those printed copies. This can be very discouraging to the small publisher. The best you can do is to try to market your book or books as professionally as possible.

A good way to learn how to do this is by subscribing to *The Huenefeld Report*. Each issue of this fortnightly 4-page newsletter is devoted to a different aspect of the book publishing business: "How to get maximum attention from the book reviewers," "What a book cover is supposed to do," "Effective mail order tactics for small book publishers," etc.

Much of the information is common knowledge (or should be) in mid-town Manhattan, but unknown to amateurs. For example, what is an acceptable schedule of discounts in the book trade? (See the issue of 18 April 1977.) What percentage of return should one reasonably hope for from a magazine advertisement? (7 March 1977.) How does one prepare a chart to forecast sales? (13 June 1977.)

If you have specific problems, you might consider requesting Huenefeld's back issue list and ordering only those issues that seem to have the answers ($2 each, $1 each to subscribers).

MAGAZINE PUBLISHING MANAGEMENT: *A practical guide to modern magazine publishing.*
Compiled by the editors of Folio: The Magazine for Magazine Management.
Folio Magazine Publishing Corporation
125 Elm St, P.O. Box 697
New Canaan CT 06840
320 pages; $29.95

This is a book for the big boys and girls. If you're really planning on becoming another Henry Luce or Hugh Hefner rather than the publisher of a poetry journal, it is an absolute must.

Nowhere in this book will you find a discussion on how to fold anything as small as an 8½ x 11" sheet of paper; instead, you'll read something like this: "Calculating Paper Usage/A Short-Cut Method. Multiply the factors listed below by the square-inch total of the sheet size you are using. *Example*: The equivalent sheet you are using in web printing is 22-1/2" x 34" equalling 765 square inches. Multiplying the 45# paper factor (.09474) by 765" will reveal that 1,000 copies of a 16-page signature (8-3/8" x 10-7/8" trim size) will require 72.476 pounds of paper."

Most of the book is far from being that technical, but it is concerned with the *business* of publishing a magazine rather than the *fun* of it. It is divided into eight major sections: 1, Starting the New Magazine; 2, Management/Finance; 3, Editorial; 4, Advertising Sales; 5, Graphics; 6, Circulation/Fulfillment; 7, Production/Printing/Paper; and 8, Promotion.

The authors of the 96 articles (compiled from the pages of *Folio*) are all successful executives and consultants — specialists in their fields — and one wonders why they seem to be so willing to share their expertise with potential competitors and clients. To promote themselves?

John Peter, former art director at *McCalls* and an editor at *Life*, and now a publications consultant, discusses among other things, the writing of headlines, the selection of logotypes, and the printing of editorial pages in black and white vs. color. A number of articles were written by Jim Kobak (A management consultant) including "The life cycle of a magazine," "Long-range planning," and "Vertical integration: The fallacy of a management concept."

Other articles touch on virtually every aspect of magazine management from "The fine art of soliciting printers' bid" by Bert Paolucci to "The rules of the circulation game" by J. Wendell Forbes to "Recruiting salespeople" by Frederic C. Decker.

THE PUBLISH-IT-YOURSELF HANDBOOK:
literary tradition & how-to
Edited by Bill Henderson
The Pushcart Book Press
P.O. Box 845
Yonkers NY 10701
362 pages; paper, $5.00; cloth, $10.00

Anyone who has thought about publishing a book or magazine, and who can read this book without being inspired to actually go out and do it, wasn't serious about being a publisher in the first place.

From Anais Nin to Stewart Brand (*Whole Earth Catalog*) Bill Henderson has put together a collection of essays that make your publishing dreams seem as though they just might come true — in spite of the recountings of some very disappointing ventures (Such as Luke Walton's description of how the self-publication of his novel *The Galapagos Kid* eventually cost him $10,873.50). The *Handbook* itself is self-published and is now in its eighth printing!

Among the 28 essays is a devastating expose by Martin Baron of the vanity (subsidy) publishing racket; Patrick Royce's success story of his perennial good-seller (it's not a best-seller, but it's not bad either) *Sailing Illustrated;* Daisy Aldan's adventures, "Poetry & a One-Woman Press;" and an interview with Barbara Garson, author and self-publisher of *MacBird* which eventually sold over 400,000 copies in the self-published and Grove Press editions.

Other well-known names from the world of small presses whose essays appear are Richard Kostelanetz, Richard Morris, Dick Higgins, and Alan Swallow. Swallow is everybody's grandfather in the contemporary small press movement, just as Harry Smith (*The Smith*) is everybody's uncle, and Len Fulton (*Small Press Review*) is everybody's big brother. Fulton also has an essay included.

In addition to the essays, a how-to section offers some practical tips and a bibliography lists seventy books about related subjects such as printing, writing, and copyediting.

Highly recommended.

PUTTING YOUR SCHOOL PAPER TO BED
Multigraphics Division
A-M Corporation
1800 West Central Rd.
Mt. Prospect IL 60056
32 pages; free on request

Some general hints for high school journalists — and, of course, plugs for Multilith and VariTyper products. The pamphlet contains a good glossary with a lot of strictly newspaper terms.

SELF PUBLICATION OF BOOKLETS & PAMPHLETS
By Malcolm Payne
Poets Vigilantes Publications
4, Wealden Close
Crowborough, Sussex, England, TN6 2ST
4 pages; mimeograph; no price given

This is a handy little pamphlet for British poets who wish to publish their own work. It has tips on the least expensive way to prepare copy for mimeograph, offset and letterpress along with full instructions for obtaining a British copyright and inclusion in the monthly, semiannual and annual editions of the *National British Bibliography*.

Mr. Payne, an active member of England's small press movement, is also author of *Poets — Why Pay to Publish?* (P V Publications, 45p), an instructional handbook for the aspiring/emerging poet that contains an expose of the vanity press (British style) along with many pointers on how to write and submit poetry to little mags.

REFERENCE BOOKS FOR EDITORS

There are certain conventions regarding English usage, grammar, punctuation, and spelling that most editors wish to follow. No matter how unconventional you may think yourself, no matter how different and avant garde you may think your magazine, you should try to stick to established rules unless you break them *intentionally* — which you can't do unless you know them. There's a great deal of difference between nonconformity and sloppiness. You'll also need reference books in which to check facts. The following books can guide the careful editor.

BREWER'S DICTIONARY OF PHRASE & FABLE
By E. Cobham Brewer
Harper & Row
10 East 53rd St.
New York NY 10022
Revised Edition
1175 Pages; cloth, $15.00

First published in 1870, this book is, as the dust jacket claims, "a gold mine of hard-to-find information — the familiar and unfamiliar in phrase, fable, romance, archaeology, history, religion, the arts, the sciences. . . " This revised and updated version was edited by Ivor H. Evans.

If, in the course of your editorial duties, you wonder at a writer's use of the phrase, "to eat the leek," there is probably no other reference book but Brewer's in which you can look it up. Where else could you learn that a "bridled bear" referred to a young nobleman under the control of a travelling tutor? That "Dirty Dick's" is a tavern in Bishopsgate, London, noted for the depth of its dust? That the duc de Richelieu invented mayonnaise when he mixed together what food was available after capturing Port Mahon, Minorca, in 1756?

The book is a handy place for looking up the stories behind mythological characters, customs, holidays, slang words, nicknames, literary characters, etc.

Hardly a necessary book, but one that's fun to own.

CBS NEWS ALMANAC
Hammon Almanac, Inc.
Maplewood NJ 07040
1,040 pages; cloth, $5.95; paper, $3.75

Who was Millard Fillmore's Attorney General? Were there any Vietnam War Medal of Honor winners from South Dakota? Where was Gene Kelly born? In what year? What were the vocations of the signers of the Declaration of Independence? Who won the women's 80-meter hurdles in the 1948 Olympics? What is the address of the National Skeet Shooting Association? What is the name of the tallest building in Boston? What is the ZIP code for Bangor, Maine? What is the student-teacher ratio of Paducah Community College? Whose picture is on a $5,000 bill?

And on and on and on.

COLLEGIATE DICTIONARIES
Webster's New Collegiate Dictionary
C & G Merriam
47 Federal St.
Springfield MA 01101
$8.95
Random House Collegiate Dictionary
201 E. 50th St.
New York NY 10022
$8.95
American Heritage Dictionary of the English Language
American Heritage
1221 Ave. of the Americas
New York NY 10036
$9.95

Take your choice, but every editor ought to have, at the very least, a "collegiate" dictionary. The Merriam-Webster has been around the longest of the three and can be found in used book stores and Goodwills. Even an edition as old as the Fourth (1931) is better than a lot of newer but cheaper dictionaries. If you can't find a used collegiate — and can't afford a new one — pick up a copy of *The Merriam-Webster Pocket Dictionary* (found even in newsstands) as a fill-in until you can get a collegiate.

THE COLUMBIA-VIKING DESK ENCYCLOPEDIA
The Viking Press
625 Madison Ave.
New York NY 10022
2 vols; 1,477 pages

Nothing can replace a good set of encyclopedias for general reference, but for handy quick reference this two-volume set will certainly suffice. It's the place to go for dates, short biographies, geographic descriptions, and more complete definitions than a dictionary will give of many words.

Used copies abound.

THE COMPACT EDITION OF THE OXFORD ENGLISH DICTIONARY
Oxford University Press
200 Madison Ave.
New York NY 10016
2 vols; 4,134 pages; $95.00

A well-known poet once wrote that when he seriously decided to devote himself to poetry, he sold his library and reinvested the money in a 13-volume set of the *Oxford English Dictionary* (which now sells new for $395).

If you too are convinced that you must have this famous dictionary, you can buy it much more cheaply. The 16,569 pages have been reduced photographically and reprinted, four-to-the-page, in just two volumes containing 4,134 pages. The reduced type is difficult to read, so each set comes complete with its own magnifying glass stored in a special drawer in the slipcase.

There's no need to spend even the more modest $95 list price for the set. The Book-of-the-Month Club (Camp Hill PA 17012) regularly advertises it as an introductory offer for just $17.50. You can use the $77.50 savings to fulfill your obligation to buy four more selections and add such books as *The Book of Lists* and Edwin Newman's *Civil Tongue* to your reference library.

A DICTIONARY OF MODERN ENGLISH USAGE
By H. W. Fowler
Oxford University Press
200 Madison Avenue
New York NY 10016
742 Pages; $10.00

In spite of this book's being considered the ultimate authority on word usage, it is not the easiest to read. There are a few reasons for this; one being that Fowler often used only the initial of a main entry when repeating it in the text. Another space-saving device also breaks the reader's stride: the use of & instead of *and*. (Perhaps it was he who encouraged this cute habit among third-rate poets and not E. E. Cummings after all.) The main problem, though, is simply that he packed a great deal of information in every sentence. One cannot "skim" Fowler and understand what he wrote.

Probably his most famous entry is that on split infinitives, which begins: "The English-speaking world may be divided into (1) those who neither know nor care what a split infinitive is; (2) those who do not know, but care very much; (3) those who know & condemn; (4) those who know & approve; & (5) those who know & distinguish . . . Those who neither know nor care are the vast majority, & are a happy folk, to be envied by most of the minority classes . . ."

Many of the word usages are strictly Britannicisms (Fowler considered Briticism a barbarous expression) and, unless you're trying to impress some British friends, they can be overlooked. When in doubt, however, take Fowler's advice.

For all his apparent snottiness, he effectively punctures much of the bloated writing that *still* prevades the printed page (the book was first published in the U.S. in 1944). He gives more examples of bad usage than good, and this negative information is actually better than positive (which is open-ended) because it sets limits.

This is an essential book and, since it has been around so long and has had so many printings, turns up frequently in used book stores and Goodwill and Salvation Army outlets.

THE ELEMENTS OF STYLE
By William Strunk, Jr.
The Macmillan Company
866 3rd Ave.
New York NY
71 pages; cloth, $4.00; paper, $1.65

Everybody recommends this book so it must be good. Actually it is pretty good: 71 pages "devoted to the cause of lucid English prose." One *is* disappointed to find typographical errors in a book of this kind ("Satifsactory," "in sort supply"). It was first published in 1918 and revised in 1959 by E. B. White who added a final chapter on attaining a personal writing style.

Strunk's portion of the book is concerned with what is correct, or acceptable, in the use of English. If you don't already know that a participial phrase at the beginning of a sentence must refer to the grammatical subject, then you should own this book. It's a popular item in used book stores.

ENCYCLOPEDIA OF THE GREAT QUOTATIONS
By George Seldes
Pocket Books
630 5th Ave.
New York NY 10020
Paper, $2.95

FAMILIAR QUOTATIONS
By John Bartlett
Citadel Press
222 Park Ave. S.
New York NY 10003
Paper, $2.95

There are many instances when others have already said what you want to say, only they've said it better. Why not quote them? And there are times when a person's character can be illustrated by quoting him or her. These are just two ways in which a book of quotations comes in handy.

The most popular of all such books is Bartlett's, but if you want some really provocative quotes by the likes of Albert Einstein, Hitler, Jefferson, Veblen, J. Edgar Hoover, Kierkegaard, etc., George Seldes is the compiler for you.

Bartlett does have a much superior index. Both books have about 200 entries under *Truth*, for example. In Bartlett's index each entry has a few key words ("man never harmed by," "sanctified by," "stranger than fiction") followed by the number of the page on which you'll find the complete quote. Some editions even have each quote on every page identified by a letter code to make finding them even easier. Seldes, on the other hand, merely lists the 200 quoted authors (each followed by one or more page numbers) beneath the heading with no clue at all as to what the person *said* about Truth. As frustrating as this can sometimes be, it gives the reader an excuse for browsing among some of the most exciting quotes ever assembled in one book.

Perhaps one day Lyle Stuart (the original publisher) will pay someone to compile a proper index for the book and then republish it.

HARPER DICTIONARY OF CONTEMPORARY USAGE
By William and Mary Morris
Harper & Row
10 East 53rd St.
New York NY 10022
731 Pages; $15.00

William Morris is Editor-in-Chief of *The American Heritage Dictionary*. Mary Morris is co-author with him of *Dictionary of Word and Phrase Origins*. Between them they know a lot about words and how to use them. As with other usage books the entries are divided among those that distinguish between pairs of words often confused (flout and flaunt, nauseous and nauseated, etc.), definitions of new, uncommon, misused, and slang words and phrases, and short essays on (usually) improper usage of the language. Many of the entries were precipitated by readers' responses to the authors' newspaper column, "Words, Wit and Wisdom."

What makes this particular dictionary different from others is that a number of words and phrases have been submitted to a panel of 136 well-known and respected writers and editors ranging from Isaac Asimov to Walter Cronkite to Barbara Tuchman to Judith Viorst. Their responses have been tabulated and their comments recorded.

One entry, for example, has to do with use of "anymore" as a synonym for "nowadays" (as in "We don't do that anymore."). Only 9% of the panel would use it in speaking, and only 4% in writing. Some of the comments were, "Barbaric patois." (John Ciardi), "What in hell is wrong with 'nowadays'?" (Stephen H. Fritchman), "This usage is standard in Dutchess County, N. Y. I have never been able to learn why." (Richard H. Rovere). None of them seemed to have considered the fact that there were certainly purists who despaired for the English language when "nowadays" gained currency during the 14th century. No matter. We're concerned here with prejudices, not logic.

Another entry had to do with the word "diction" which means "choice of words" and not, as it is currently employed, "enunciation." 61% agreed that *diction* now has both meanings, equally acceptable. 39% felt that the distinction should be observed. "I'm hopeless here because I went to a school where Voice and Diction was a required course — it bears the academic stamp of approval for me." (Walter Kerr). "Webster II thinks so, but I don't." (Rex Stout). "Yes. I regret this, but so it is. In singing, diction has long meant enunciation." (Lionel Trilling). And so on.

For those interested in word usage, the book is enjoyable browsing. And for those words in contention that were submitted to the panel, you can always find one "authority" to back up your pet vulgarity.

MODERN AMERICAN USAGE
By Wilson Follett
Warner Books
75 Rockefella Plaza
New York NY 10019
Paper, $1.95

If Fowler (*Modern English Usage*) can be considered the ultimate authority, Follett can be thought of as the most practical authority, at least for Americans. According to the dust jacket blurb, when Follett began to write his book in 1958 he penned these words: "It is time we had an American book of usage grounded in the philosophy that the best in language — which is often the simplest — is not too good to be aspired to." He hoped his book would be "American to the marrow," and it is. Follett died in 1963 before finishing his work. Jacques Barzun, with the cooperation of his collaborators, completed it.

The 300-odd entries are divided into four general categories: Diction (which he uses correctly, of course; see the reference to this word in the review of the *Harper Dictionary of Contemporary Usage*), Idiom, Syntax, and Style. Even without these, the introductory essays, "On Usage, Purism, and Pedantry," "On the Need of an Orderly Mind," and "On the Need of Some Grammar," are nearly worth the price of admission. If you can't buy the book, at least go to the library and read these essays (a mere 28 pages).

The entries are much easier to read than Fowler's and many of them are quite amusing. Follett does go off the deep end occasionally (as when he chides us for pronouncing margarine with a soft *g* rather than hard) but on the whole this is a collection of very sound advice for the writer and editor who want what they have written to be easily understood. (Pedants, please note: If that last sentence bothered you, read Fowler's comments on split infinitives.)

THE OXFORD DICTIONARY OF ENGLISH ETYMOLOGY
Edited by C. T. Onions
Oxford University Press
200 Madison Ave.
New York NY 10016
1024 Pages; cloth, $30.00
Strictly for word freaks.

ROGET'S INTERNATIONAL THESAURUS
T. Y. Crowell
666 5th Ave.
New York NY 10019
Cloth, $8.95
A thesaurus, for those who don't know, is a kind of backwards dictionary. It's for those instances where you know the definition of a word, but can't remember the word itself.

Suppose that in a review of someone's poetry you want to use the word *vapid* to generally describe it. You know the word exists, it's on the tip of your tongue, but you just can't think of it. All you can remember is that the word you're looking for means flat and spiritless. What you do is look up the adjective *flat* in the index of the thesaurus. Listed beneath *flat* are a number of words (*inert, horizontal,* etc.) and you read down the list until you come to *insipid*. That's not quite, but is almost, the word you want. You follow the reference number printed after *insipid* (which happens to be 391.2) to that section of the book. And sure enough, there you find *vapid*. It rings a bell immediately, and you've just relearned a word.

You also find the word *jejune* listed there. Should you use it instead? Yes, if it's already part of your vocabulary and conveys precisely the meaning you want. And here's the danger in using a thesaurus: the temptation to employ a word you've never used before just to show off.

No two words are exactly synonymous, and if you use an unfamiliar word it might very well have the wrong connotation. It will be obvious to your readers that you are writing beyond your vocabulary.

UNABRIDGED DICTIONARIES

Webster's Third New International
G & C Marriam
47 Federal St.
Springfield MA 01101
$59.95

Random House Dictionary of the English Language
201 E. 59th St.
New York NY 10022
$35.00

As useful as an unabridged dictionary is, you'd be much better off to buy a well-known "collegiate" dictionary than some off-brand unabridged. (Just because it has "Webster's" in the title doesn't mean that it's going to be any good.)

If you do buy a good unabridged dictionary, be prepared to spend another $50 or so for a movable stand to put it on. Otherwise you'll end up breaking the spine in a couple of years because of excessive handling. (The Merriam-Webster weighs over 13 pounds!)

WORD WATCHER'S HANDBOOK
By Phyllis Martin
David McKay Company
750 Third Avenue
New York NY 10017
81 pages; cloth, $7.95; paper, $3.95
Archie Bunker and Mrs. Malaprop wouldn't be nearly as funny if they had read this book — and that would be our loss. But who wants to be "funny" in real life? It's embarrassing enough to discover that you've been misusing a word in conversation all these years, but when you immortalize it in print, it can embarrass you forever.

Ms. Martin has divided the book into three sections of commonly misused and abused words and phrases: a *deletionary* of cliches and needless words; a usage dictionary of everyday terms; and a pronouncing dictionary of common pitfalls (boatswain, comptroller, ennui, etc.). You are guaranteed — even during just a quick browse — to discover that you have been misusing some word or phrase.

REVIEW JOURNALS

BOOKLIST
American Library Association
50 East Huron St.
Chicago IL 60611
A standard reference for librarians.

BOOKS IN CANADA: *A national review of books*
366 Adelaide St., East.
Toronto, Ontario M5A 1N4

Approximately 3,000 English-language books are published in Canada every year. This periodical reviews about 500 of them. The odds are six-to-one against you, but that's better than the odds in most periodicals. Send them a copy.

BOOKSWEST MAGAZINE: a national monthly of the book trade

3757 Wilshire Blvd.
Los Angeles CA 90010

This is a slick journal that would like to become *Publisher's Weekly* on a monthly basis, and it may just do that. What really distinguishes it from the big weekly on the opposite coast is the attention paid to small press publications. It is filled with reviews of books published in such unlikely places as Missoula, Montana and Layton, Utah cheek by jowl with Knopf and Simon & Schuster publications. No distinction is made between BIG and little.

Like *Publisher's Weekly*, this is a trade journal with articles and ads aimed at many segments of the industry: publishers, writers, librarians, book sellers. If you've published something you think is good — book or periodical — send them a copy.

EMERGENCY LIBRARIAN!

46 Gormley Ave.
Toronto, Ontario M4V 1Z1

EL featutes a column called "Books for Liberated Children" and reviews of small Canadian presses.

HORN BOOK

585 Boylston St.
Boston MA 02116

A standard reference for librarians looking for juveniles.

KIRKUS REVIEWS

60 W. 13th St.
New York NY 10011

This is a standard library reference tool. The reviews tend to be unkind if the material warrants it, so be careful.

LIBRARY JOURNAL

1180 Avenue of the Americas
New York NY 10036

A standard reference for librarians.

THE OTTAWA CITIZEN

1101 Baxter Road
Box 5020
Ottawa, Ontario K2C 3M4

Send periodicals that you would like to have considered for a possible review to Richard Labonte.

PUBLISHER'S WEEKLY

1180 Avenue of the Americas
New York NY 10036

This is expensive, but the education you'll get from reading it for a year will be worth it if you're really serious about publishing books.

QUILL & QUIRE

59 Front Street E.
Toronto M5E 1B3 Ontario

Read by public, Elementary, high school, university, industrial and resource centre librarians, booksellers, publishers and teachers in Canada.

Send review copies of little mags to the attention of Paul Stuewe.

THE REVIEWING LIBRARIAN

Ontario School Library Association
15 Carmine Place
Guelph, Ontario N1E 3V2

Send review copies to Ken Ellis, Canadian Periodicals for Schools. Here is a good place to help expand sales to schools.

SCHOOL LIBRARY JOURNAL

1180 Avenue of the Americas
New York NY 10036

Like it's big brother (sister? sibling?) this is a standard professional journal for librarians.

SMALL PRESS REVIEW

Dustbooks
P.O. Box 1056
Paradise CA 95969
Monthly; $8.50, individuals; $13.50 institutions

The very fact that *SPR* is in its tenth year would seem to prove that there is a continuing — and growing — interest in what's being published outside of mid-town Manhattan. It is also evidence of the dedication and persistence of editor/publisher Len Fulton and his associates Ellen Ferber and Nancy Cahill. The magazine *lost* $5-6,000 a year for the first eight years of its existence.

There's a lot here: news (hard and soft), reviews, articles, announcements, analyses of the small press movement, updates of listings in the *International Directory*, letters — and some interesting ads.

In many ways, *SPR* is a trade journal not so different from *Professional Builder* and *Publishers' Weekly*. As such, it is of interest to everyone in the field, from buyers to sellers, and to those who sell to the sellers. That is, from publishers to libraries (and other buyers of small press publications) and to typesetters, printers, poets and writers. While not all small publishers and only a few garreted poets can justify $8.50 a year, they should make a point to read it in the library. If the library doesn't subscribe, they should insist that it start doing so. There's no excuse for college and university libraries not to have it on their shelves.

Every small press should keep *SPR* up-to-date on their current activities (change of address, search for contributions, special issue, etc.) and should submit review copies of everything published. They're sure to get a mention here.

Question: Are there no *bad* small press books and periodicals being published? 40 of 45 reviews in three issues were favorable; the other five "mixed" at worst. If you can't say anything nice, don't say anything at all? Maybe, but ". . . highly entertaining . . . well-written . . . simply one of the best . . . delightful . . . vibrant and alive . . . very impressive . . . thoroughly enjoyable . . . " and other nice things tend to become, as our good buddy Hamlet said, "weary, stale, flat, and unprofitable." But let not this criticism stand in the way of *this* good review.

WILSON LIBRARY BULLETIN
980 University Ave.
Bonx NY 10452
Yet another professional journal for librarians.

COPYRIGHTING

All you need to do to copyright a book or periodical is to publish it with the proper copyright notice: © 1978 by Joe Blow. If you want, you can spend $6 to register it with the Copyright Office.

First, write and ask for the proper form (explain what it is you want to copyright — book or periodical). When you receive this, just follow the instructions.

If you forget to print the notice, you'll *have* to register your printed work if you want the copyright protection. It used to be that if you forgot the notice you couldn't get a copyright. That's no longer true. The catch is that no-one can be sued for innocently reproducing your published work if you do forget the notice. Once you've registered with the Copyright Office, however, you can order publishers to stop reproducing your work, copyright notice or not.

Unpublished works can't be registered. But that's okay because they are automatically copyrighted after you've typed the first two words.

Don't waste time and money sticking a poem in an envelope and sending it to yourself by registered mail. All this proves is that you have received an envelope in the mail that *now* contains a poem. You'd be better off in court with a responsible witness who read it on its completion — or even during its composition.

For any additional information and forms write: Register of Copyrights, Library of Congress, Washington DC 20559.

Don't hire a lawyer to do any of this for you. You can do it yourself.

GRANTS AND FUNDING

THE COORDINATING COUNCIL OF LITERARY MAGAZINES
80 Eighth Ave.
New York NY 10011
The Coordinating Council of Literary Magazines (CCLM, established in 1967, is a national nonprofit organization supported by the National Endowment for the Arts, the New York State Council on the Arts, and private sources.

Grants Program: Literary magazines that are noncommercial (tax exempt status not required), that have put out at least three issues, and that have published for a least a year are eligible to apply for a CCLM grant.

Grants committees, composed of editors and writers, meet twice a year in the fall and spring. Each committee serves only once; three members are elected by CCLM members and two are appointed by the Board of Directors to help insure balanced representation.

Grants are made for general support of publication, authors' payments, and special development such as graphics, etc. Grant amounts range from $250 to $3500. On the average 250 magazines receive grants through CCLM each year; the magazines encompass a wide range of literary interests and are located throughout the United States.

Membership: CCLM membership is open to noncommercial literary magazines that have published for at least one year and put out at least three issues. There is no membership fee.

Projects: The College Contest is an annual awards program for undergraduate literary magazines. Six cash prizes are offered; the deadline for each year's contest is June 30 and the winners are announced in the fall.

The CCLM Awards program offers cash prizes annually to writers for first publication in a particular literary magazine and companion prizes to the editors who published and nominated the winning work. The program is open to CCLM members.

In February 1976, The Ford Foundation made a three year grant to CCLM for a group of pilot projects in distribution and promotion for literary magazines. The program aims to help participating magazines increase their sales and reach wider audiences.

Regional Meetings: The meetings are held twice a year in different parts of the United States to bring together editors and writers for technical and literary workshops.

Library: CCLM maintains a collection of literary magazines which may be used by the general public. About 5000 magazines dating from 1967 to the present are in the library located in the CCLM office.

Futher information about application procedures, membership, projects, and regional meetings may be obtained from the CCLM office.

Note: There are those in the world of little magazines who claim that the CCLM is a "we cosy few" organization more interested in sustaining a few well-established journals than in supporting newer, more experimental mags. Don't let this deter you from making a grant application.

STATE ARTS COUNCILS
Find the address of your state's arts council and write asking if they have any programs to provide funding for literary magazines. Some do.

INTERNATIONAL STANDARD BOOK NUMBER (ISBN)

INTERNATIONAL STANDARD SERIAL NUMBER (ISSN)

Many small press publishers regard standardization and computers and code numbers and all the other credenda of Big Business with a natural revulsion. But if you want to deal with book jobbers, subscription agencies, and university libraries, you might as well learn to live with these things.

The International Organization for Standardization, the International Center of the International Serials Data System, the International Standard Book Numbering Agency, Unesco, the French Government, the National Serials Data Program, the Library of Congress, the National Agricultural Library, the National Library of Medicine, the Bibliothque Nationale, and the R. R. Bowker Co. (Xerox), among many other agencies, have conspired to institute the ISBN and ISSN. You can try fighting them if you want.

If you'd like your periodical to have an ISSN assignment, or if you'd like every book title you publish to have its very own ISBN, write to R. R. Bowker, 1180 Avenue of the Americas, New York, N.Y. 10036, and ask them for the proper forms. (If you have your periodical listed in *Ulrich's International Periodical Directory* you'll be assigned a number whether you want it or not.)

MAILING LISTS

AMERICAN LIBRARY DIRECTORY
R. R. Bowker Co.
1180 Avenue of the Americas
New York NY 10036
$36.00
Thousands of public, college, and industrial libraries in the United States and Canada, complete with names of librarians. You can buy this annually, type the labels on sheets for reproduction on Xeroxed labels and save yourself a considerable amount of money if you plan on sending out more than one mailing a year. This way you'll have your own mailing list just as up-to-date as any you could lease.

FRITZ S. HOFHEIMER INC.
88 Third Ave.
Mineola NY 11501
Write for a catalog. It offers you a choice of almost 20,000 different lists, ranging from 767 Automobile Association of America branch offices to 24 Zwieback manufacturers. It also has Canadian lists.

LOVEJOY'S COLLEGE GUIDE
Simon & Schuster
630 5th Ave.
New York NY 10012
Paperback; $4.95
Inexpensive source of college and university names and addresses.

DIRECT MAIL LIST RATES AND DATA
Standard Rate & Data Service
5201 Old Orchard Rd.
Skokie IL 60076
Semiannual with 18 update bulletins; $60 yr.
This is the standard reference tool of the direct-mail industry. Each semi-annual edition is the size of a metropolitan phone directory.

ENCYCLOPEDIA OF ASSOCIATIONS
Gale Research Co.
Book Tower
Detroit MI 48226
Available in most libraries. A good source for specialized mailing lists. There are people listed in here who don't even know they can sell their list. They will when you approach them. (Don't pay over 5c a name.)

MICROFORM SUPPLIERS

Bell & Howell Micro-Photo Division
Old Mansfield Road
Wooster OH 44691

University Microfilms
300 N. Zeeb Road
Ann Arbor MI 48203

SUBSCRIPTION AGENCIES

Write to as many of these agencies as you can afford, informing them of your existence, and asking them for a standard rate and commission form. Ebsco, Faxon and Turner are probably the three largest, so make sure to write them. Keep track of which agencies you send information to in case you have changes in price or commission later on.

Alesco
404 Setle Drive
Paramus NJ 07652

American Magazine Services
914 Jefferson
Topeka KS 66604

Aquinas Subscription Agency
718 Pelham Blvd.
St. Paul MN 55114

Ancorp National Services, Inc.
600 East 95th St.
Kansas City MO 64131

Black Magazine Agency
Box 342
Logansport IN 46947

Blackwell's Periodicals
Oxenford House
Magdalen St.
Oxford, England OX1 3AD

Crowley, Inc.
330 East 204th St.
Bronx NY 10467

Ebsco Industries, Inc.
P.O. Box 1943
Brimingham AL 35201

Ellsworth Magazine Service
332 South Michigan
Chicago IL 60604

F. W. Faxon Co.
15 Southwest Park
Westwood MA 02090

Regineld F. Fennell
1002 W. Michigan Ave.
Jackson MI 49201

Franklin Square-Dawson
6 Thorncliffe Park Drive
Toronto, Canada

Fusao Taniguchi
62 Funchal St.
Honolulu HI 96812

Victor Hansen
Bruunsgade 45
DK - 8000 Aarhus C
Denmark

Instructor Subscription Agency
Instructor Park
Danville NY 14437

Maxwell International
Fairview Park
Elsmford NY 10523

McGregor Magazine Agency
Mt. Morris IL 61054

Moore-Cottrell
North Cohocton NY 14868

National Organization Service
401 Shops Building
Des Moines IA 50309

Olympic Periodical Agency
909 S. 28th St.
Tacoma WA 98409

Walter Peck Agency
Bank of Galesburg Bldg.
Galesburg IL 61401

Popular Subscription
P.O. Box 1566
Terre Haute IN 47808

Publications Unlimited
P.O. Box 100
Boynton Beach FL 33435

Leigh M. Railsback
1276 North Lake Ave.
Pasadena CA 91104

The Rayner Agency
100 East Chicago St.
Elgin IL 60120

Read More Publications
140 Cedar St.
New York NY 10006

Research Services Corporation
P.O. Drawer 16549
Forth Worth TX 76133

Southwest Business Publications
12633 Memorial Drive
Suite 33
Houston TX 77024

Squire Magazine Agency
6009 Pinewood Road
Oakland CA 94611

Stechert-Macmillan, Inc.
7250 Westfield Ave.
Pennsauken NJ 08110

Turner Subscription Agency
235 Park Ave. South
New York NY 10003

Universal Periodical Service
2500 Packard Road
Ann Arbor MI 48104

Vancouver Magazine Service, Ltd.
3455 Gardner Court
Burnaby, BC Canada V5G 3K8

W. R. Watson and Staff
1181 Euclid Ave.
Berkely VA 94708

TOOLS FOR THE GRAPHIC ARTIST

CLIP ART

Various companies sell camera-ready line art. Usually, it looks like camera-ready line art, but lots of people like it anyway. A good source for borders, backgrounds, mortices, etc. Most of the companies will offer specials or give you samples if you place a small order. Take advantage of these if you're planning on buying any. Write for catalogs.

Dynamic Graphics, Inc.
6705 N. Sheridan Rd.
Peoria IL 61614

Harry R. Volk Art Studio
P.O. Box 4098
Rockford IL 61110

D'Artiste Associates
P.O. Box 3444
Bridgeport CT 06600

Forward Graphics
2 9th St.
DesMoines IA 50309
   When writing to Forward Graphics for information, make sure to mention that you *do not* want them to mail you anything on approval (unless, of course, you do). Otherwise, you'll be stuck with sending back an unwanted package of material — or paying an invoice of $75 or so.

DOVER PICTORIAL ARCHIVE SERIES

Dover Publications, Inc.
180 Varick St.
New York NY 10014
   Here is a good source of out-of-copyright steel engravings and wood cuts, and new original drawings that may be reproduced without further permission (in limited quantities for each project — Dover doesn't want you reproducing an entire book at one time). They are inexpensive ($I.50 and up) and nice to have. Write asking for details.

GRAPHIC ARTS SUPPLIES

   Waxers, layout sheets, steel rules, pens, brushes, light tables — everything you need to set up shop. Write for catalogs.

Dick Blick
P.O. Box 1267
Galesburg IL 61401

CCM Arts & Crafts, Inc.
9520 Baltimore Ave.
College Park MD 20740

Midwest Publishers Supply Co.
4640 N. Olcott Ave.
Chicago IL 60656
(The best single source for strictly graphic arts supplies: Olfa knives, layout sheets, border tapes, non-reproducing blue pencils, waxers, etc.)

MASKING FILM

Separon Co., Inc.
56 W. 22nd St.
New York NY 10018

Ulano
210 East 86th St.
New York NY 10018

TRANSFER LETTERING, BORDERS, BEN DAY SHADING FILMS

   Write for catalogs, asking for the name of the dealer nearest you. In some cases, they may be willing to sell to you direct.

Artype
345 E. Terra Cotta Ave.
Crystal Lake IL 60014

Chartpak
1 River Rd.
Leeds MA 01053

Heidelberg Easter Inc.
73-45 Woodhaven Blvd.
Glendale NY 11227

Letraset
33 New Bridge Rd.
Bergenfield NJ 07621

Pressure Graphics, Inc.
1725 Armitage Ct.
Addison IL 60101
   This is almost certainly the least expensive transfer lettering you can buy (only $1.50 a sheet). They do have a minimum $15 order policy but when you figure that you can get 10 sheets for the same price it would cost you to buy only four sheets from another company, you won't mind.

Prestype, Inc.
194 Veterans Blvd.
Carlstadt NJ 07027

Richard Schlatter Design
265 Capital Ave., N.E.
Battle Creek MI 49017

Zipatone
150 Fencl Lane
Hillside IL 60162

UNITED STATES POSTAL SERVICE

   All publishers have a love/hate relationship with the Postal Service: they know they can't survive without it, and sometimes they think they can't survive with it. The fact is, the service isn't all that bad, and if one is acquainted with the various classes of mail and rate structures, one can save money and get even better service.
   There are no rates given in the following descriptions; many of them would be out-of-date on the day this book is published. All post offices have current rate cards available.

FIRST CLASS
   The standard of service for this class of mail is supposed to be overnight within the local area. The Postal Service defines the local area as the

entire section center of orgin — that is, all post offices that have the same first three numbers in the ZIP code as the post office at which a piece is mailed. Overnight delivery, it is claimed, will also be made to adjacent sectional centers. Outside the local area and up to 600 miles, the standard is second day delivery. Within the contiguous 48 states, the standard is third day. (These standards are for pieces mailed before 5 p.m.). They make no claims for Alaska or Hawaii.

Mail that must be sent First Class includes handwritten and typewritten messages, bills, checks (cancelled or not), forms that have been filled in, and greeting cards.

The minimum dimensions for First Class are 3x4¼". Postcards exceeding 4¼x6" require postage at the rate for letters.

The First Class rate is always lower per ounce after the first ounce. If, for example, the basic rate is 15¢ for the first ounce and 13 for each additional ounce, don't put three 13¢ stamps on a three-ounce letter. Frequent users of the mail can save a few dollars a year by buying a sheet of 13¢ stamps (or whatever the current rate is) to have on hand. For every sheet you use, you have saved $2 over what you would have spent had you not purchased them.

If you are sending out many identical pieces of First Class mail it is possible to save money by pre-sorting and bundling. This isn't hard to do, and your mailing list ought to be in ZIP code order anyway. Check with your postmaster for the conditions required for this savings.

Forwarding, Return, and Address Correction

One of the advantages of First Class mail is that it is forwarded, if possible, to the new address or else returned to the sender at no additional charge.

If you suspect that an addressee has moved and would like to know the new address, mark the mail "Address Correction Requested — Use Form 3547." You will be charged a small amount for the new address, if known. If it is unforwardable, the piece will be returned to you at no charge.

If you are just checking on an address, but do not want the piece forwarded, mark it "Address Correction Requested — Do Not Forward." Again, a small fee will be charged only if the new address is known.

Postcards will be forwarded at no charge to the new address if it is known. Otherwise, they are destroyed. If you think an addressee has moved, make sure to mark the postcard "Return Postage Guaranteed" or else it may be destroyed and you never will know what happened.

FIRST CLASS PRIORITY MAIL

This class is for packages weighing over 16 ounces for which you are willing to pay a premium rate in order to get First Class delivery standards rather than parcel post standards.

Check the current Priority rate and you may discover that it would be cheaper to get the same service by sending the package Fourth Class Special Handling, *q.v.*

FIRST CLASS ENCLOSED

When including a typed or handwritten message in a package there is no need to pay the First Class rate on the entire weight. For example, if a manuscript is being mailed with a cover letter, weigh the package, determine the Special Fourth Class postage, then add the postage for one ounce of First Class mail. In addition to the Fourth Class markings on the package, mark "First Class Enclosed."

FIRST CLASS BUSINESS REPLY

These are the cards and envelopes that are distributed for use by mailers in sending mail to the original distributor without prepayment of postage. The distributor pays only if a piece is returned.

This permit used to be free and the rate quite reasonable. All that has changed. The permit fee is now expensive and the rate high. Most companies that sell by direct mail still feel that it is worth providing a potential customer with a postage-free card or envelope to encourage impulsive purchases. Not everyone has a postage stamp on hand and by the time they get one the urge to buy may be gone.

SECOND CLASS

Only newspapers and magazines that have a regular frequency of publication can qualify for this class of mail. The rate is very inexpensive compared to other classes. Mimeographed or spirit-duplicated periodicals do not qualify, nor do publications designed primarily for free circulation or sold at only a token rate.

The major problem with Second Class mail for the nonprofessional is that it is very difficult to process. The editorial contents and the advertising portions are paid for at different rates, and the advertising postage rate is determined by the distance of the addressee from the mailer. There are other complications.

What any publisher must do before making the decision to apply for a Second Class Permit is to sit down with someone at the local post office and have a long talk. Even at that, and armed with pamphlets and printed regulations, processing the first mailing will be a confusing and frustrating experience. Eventually it becomes routine and is well worth the effort.

SECOND CLASS TRANSIENT

A mailer other than the publisher can mail individual, complete copies of a publication at the Transient Rate or at the Special Fourth Class rate, whichever is lower.

THIRD CLASS MAIL SINGLE PIECES

This is a class of mail often overlooked by individuals. Circulars, booklets, catalogs, newsletters, corrected proof sheets, photographs, printed drawings and merchandise qualify.

Each piece of Third Class mail is limited to less than 16 ounces. The same material weighing 16 ounces or more is classified as fourth class, or parcel post, mail. Many people when mailing something less than a pound send it by more expensive First Class rate when they could save money by using Third.

THIRD CLASS BULK MAIL

Irregularly published periodicals and direct-mail advertisers can take advantage of this rate as long as they mail in quantities over 200 pieces or 50 pounds at a time.

There's an initial fee and a yearly fee, but the rate is low enough (about 60% of First Class) to more than make up for this expense. Processing is much simpler than with Second Class. Again, this requires a talk with a postal employee who is a specialist in this area.

THIRD CLASS NON-PROFIT

This is a super rate if you can get it, and a number of little mags have managed to do so. The problem in getting it is not with the postal service but the IRS. If you have a bona fide non-profit organization incorporated under the laws of your state, you can plan on as many as two years passing from the time you apply for federal non-profit status until the day you actually get it — or are turned down.

Before drawing up your articles of incorporation, stop by the post office for a Form 3624. This will give you some hints for writing your statement of purpose which, if not worded just right, can disqualify you as far as the IRS is concerned. And without the IRS imprimatur, you can't get the non-profit mailing permit. It would be best, if possible, to visit an IRS office before filing incorporation papers.

FOURTH CLASS MAIL (PARCEL POST) AND UNITED PARCEL SERVICE

This is for packages that weigh over 16 ounces. The rate is determined by the weight of the package and the distance it is to travel.

If you're sending more than one package during a single week, you might consider using United Parcel Service instead. (UPS charges a $2 fee for one week's service in addition to shipping charges.) Unlike the Postal Service, they will come to your house or place of business to pick up the packages.

Look up the United Parcel Service number in your phone book. If the call-in number is in a distant city, you can probably call collect. Ask for Customer Service. Tell the person who answers that you would like to ship some packages. Have the following information ready when you call: weight of each package (not to exceed 50 pounds each), size of the packages (not to exceed 108 inches in girth and length*), and addresses of the packages' destinations. They will have to know ZIP codes for figuring the rate since UPS uses the same zone system as the Postal Service.

You cannot ship more than 100 pounds to one address in one day. If you have over 100 pounds,

---

* The term "girth and length" sometimes confuses people. Stand the package so that the longest dimension is from floor to ceiling. Then measure it as you would measure your waist and height. Add these figures together.

separate the packages into two or more shipments to be picked up on succeeding days.

After giving the shipping information to UPS, you will be told the charges (which will include the $2 weekly fee in the first day's pickup charge) so that you can have a check ready when the man comes the following day. They will also tell you, over the phone, the receipt number of the transaction. Make sure to note this on the check and to keep it in your records in case of non-delivery. The charges include $50 insurance on each package. If you want more it is available at a reasonable rate.

NOTE: UPS will *not* take responsibility for original artwork or paste-ups. If you want to take your chances and ship it anyway, tell them it's "printed matter."

SPECIAL FOURTH CLASS RATE — BOOKS (OR MANUSCRIPT, etc.)

A book must have 24 pages of which at least 22 are printed. Also included are films of 16 mm or narrower, printed music either bound or in sheet form, sound recordings, playscripts, manuscripts, and looseleaf pages and binders containing medical information.

Mark the package "Special Fourth Class Rate" plus a description of the item, such as "Books" or "Printed Music."

This rate is getting higher and higher, but it is still considerably lower than Parcel Post or United Parcel Service.

FOURTH CLASS LIBRARY RATE

This is another super rate but is available only for interlibrary mailing (except for a few certain articles — not books) mailed by individuals to libraries.

FOURTH CLASS CATALOGS

There are special rates for single copies of catalogs (that do not quality for Book Rate) that weigh over 16 ounces each.

FOURTH CLASS BULK RATE

If you mail over 300 copies at one time of a catalog weighing more than 16 ounces, there is a special permit with a very low rate available.

SPECIAL DELIVERY

This mail is delivered as soon as practicable after it arrives at the addressee's post office. It virtually assures delivery on the day received at that post office but does not speed up transportation time from the point of origin. You can use Special Delivery with any class of mail.

SPECIAL HANDLING

This small extra fee will give preferential handling to Third and Fourth Class mail, generally resulting in its being delivered as quickly as first class mail. On heavy packages, a better deal than Priority Mail.

CERTIFIED MAIL

All this does is guarantee that a piece of mail has been delivered and signed for. It is primarily for items which have no particular money value.

The Postal Service will keep a record of the delivery and, for an extra fee, will give a copy of the receipt to the sender.

REGISTERED MAIL

This is for sending valuables (limit of indemnity $10,000) and to guarantee that the mail is put into the hands of the person for whom it is intended. Registered Mail is transported separately from other mail and kept under lock.

INTERNATIONAL REPLY COUPON

These are great when sending a manuscript to a foreign country. The publisher receiving the manuscript would like to have a stamped, addressed envelope enclosed. But you don't know where to buy Bolivian or Greek stamps. Go to your post office and buy three or four International Reply Coupons and enclose them with your ms. The recipient will be able to take these to a local post office and exchange them for native stamps. Each coupon is exchangeable for stamps representing the postage for an ordinary letter of the first weight step sent by surface to a foreign country. Three or four coupons would cover the cost of returning most manuscripts.

Glossary

bkh

Acetate Overlay

A clear plastic sheet placed over artwork on which additional art or type can be added for superimposing or color separation.

Address Correction Requested

A line added to the face of bulk mail pieces asking the Postal Service to return, for a fee, any mail that is undeliverable because addressee has moved, and to indicate, if known, the new address.

Adhesive

Paste, glue, wax, rubber cement.

Advance

Money paid to an author prior to publication, and to be subtracted from future royalties.

Agate

1. A small size of type approximately 5½ points.

2. A printer's measure equal to 1/14 of an inch by one column wide used principally by advertising agencies and newspapers.

3. A burnisher used by bookbinders.

Airbrush

An adjustable instrument operated by compressed air and used to apply ink or paint.

Aperture

The lens opening of a camera or enlarger.

Appendix

Supplemental material published at the end of a book.

Artwork

A general term used to describe copy that has been prepared for reproduction.

Ascender

That part of a lower case letter that extends above the main part of the letter.

Audited Circulation

A periodical's circulation that has been verified by an outside agency.

Autograph Party

A sales event in a retail establishment at which the author of a book is present to sign copies.

Back Issue or Number

An out-of-date issue of a periodical.

Benday

A dotted, lined, or otherwise textured screen.

Binding

That which holds the pages and cover of a book or periodical together.

Blanket

The rubber surface of an offset press from which the ink is transferred to the material being printed.

Blanket Cylinder

The drum on which the blanket is held in position.

Bleed

Printing extending beyond the trim size of printed material thereby eliminating a margin.

Blind Embossing

A relief impression on paper that remains unprinted.

Blow-in Card

Usually a Business Reply Card inserted in a periodical but not bound in.

Blowup

A photographic enlargement.

Blurb

A paragraph or sentence extolling the virtues of a book or periodical.

Body Copy

The text of a publication or advertisement.

Body Type

The type used for the text.

Bold Face

Heavy type.

Border

A printed line, either plain or ornamental.

BRC,BRE

Business Reply Card, Business Reply Envelope

Brochure

A pamphlet of 4 or more pages, usually containing material of an informative nature.

Broken Font

A typesetting film or mat that produces an incomplete letter.

Bulk

The relative thickness of bound pages.

Bulk Contract

An agreement by which an advertiser promises to purchase an agreed upon number of column inches or agate lines within a given period of time.

Bulk Rate

1. The rate per column inch or agate line that an advertiser pays under a Bulk Contract.

2. The rate for sending mail using a 2nd or 3rd class permit.

Bullet
Dots used in text or a series of lines to emphasize the beginnings of new lines.

Business Reply Card, Business Reply Envelope
A card or envelope for which the addressee has made arrangements with the Postal Service to pay the postage if mailed.

Calendar Art
Unsophisticated paintings or drawings with popular appeal.

Calender
To press paper between rollers to make smooth.

Callout
A number (with accompanying legend) or word placed directly on a drawing to identify a constituent part of the object drawn.

Camera-ready
Finished artwork.

Cancellation
The early termination of a subscription to a periodical.

Caps
Uppercase or capital letters.

Caption
The words beneath a photo or drawing describing the contents of the picture.

Carbon Ribbon
Typewriter ribbon that can be used only once, and that prints especially sharp and reproducible type.

Cash With Copy
Payment made for printing or advertising that is paid when placing a definite order.

Center Spread or Center Fold
The sheet containing the two pages in the very middle of a saddle-stitched publication.

Chap Book
A small book of poetry.

Character Count
Estimating the type to be set by actually counting the number of letters.

Chase
The metal frame used to hold type for letterpress printing.

Cheshire Label
Specially prepared address labels, relatively inexpensive, that are mechanically applied to mailing pieces.

Circulation
The number of copies sold per issue of a periodical.

Classified Advertising
Small ads without illustration arranged categorically on a page.

Clip Art
Commercially prepared and non-exclusive artwork sold camera-ready.

Close-up
A photo taken with the camera very close to the subject.

Close-up lens
A lens attachment that permits a photo to be taken at a closer distance than the camera lens would allow.

Clothbound
A rigid book cover of cloth-covered bindery board.

Cold Type
Type set by any method other than metal type.

Collate
The assembly of printed pages into their proper order for binding.

Colophon
1. An inscription placed at the end of a book containing facts relative to the book's production.
2. An identifying mark or symbol of a printer or publisher.

Color Separation
The photographic division of multi-colored art into basic colors for reproduction on a printing press.

Column
A standardized vertical arrangement of printed matter on a page.

Column Width
The width of a column, usually measured in picas.

Composition
1. The arrangement of elements within a photograph.
2. Typesetting.

Computer Type
Type set photographically by any of various computer-operated techniques.

Condensed Type
A type face narrower than it is usually printed.

Contact Print
A photographic print made by holding the negative tightly against the paper.

Contact Screen
A plastic sheet with a usually dotted or textured pattern used in direct contact with a film or plate to transform a continuous tone picture into a halftone or to give a tonal value.

Continuous Tone
An unscreened photo or drawing in which there are gradations in tone from the lightest to the darkest.

Contrast
The range in extremes between the darkest and lightest portions of a picture.

Controlled Circulation
Distribution at no charge of a publication to individuals or companies on the basis of their title or occupation.

Co-op Mailing
A mailing in which two or more advertisements are enclosed in one envelope with the cost of the mailing shared by the participants.

Copy
1. Typewritten material submitted to a printer for composition.
2. Body Copy.
3. Material written for advertising.

Copy-dot
The method by which previously screened art is rephotographed without rescreening to achieve a halftone.

Copy-editing
The final reading and correcting of material to be submitted to a printer.

Copy Fitting
Estimating the amount of space needed to set written material in a given size and style of type.

Copyright
The legal method of securing publishing rights to printed matter.

Copywriter
A writer of advertising copy.

Cover Paper or Stock
The paper, usually heavier than that used for pages, to cover a book or periodical.

CPM
Cost per thousand.

Crop Marks
Indications of the finished size of a picture.

Script

Cursive
A typeface that imitates handwriting.

Cut
A small drawing or metal plate used in printing.

Cyan
One of the three basic color inks used in full-color printing. (Blue)

Darkroom
A light-tight area used for processing film and photographic paper.

Deadbeat
A subscriber to a periodical who does not pay.

Deadline
The time set for the completion of work.

Dealer Discount
The percentage of an item's price that is the seller's commission.

Deckle Edge
Rough untrimmed paper.

Decorative Type
Type designed not so much for readability as for special effects.

Delete
The term commonly used in the printing trade to indicate that something be removed from copy.

Demographics
The socio-economic characteristics of those residing in a geographic location.

Depth of Field
The distance between the nearest and farthest subjects that appear in reasonable focus in a photograph.

Descender
That part of a lower case letter that extends below the main part of the letter.

Desensitizer
A solution for processing offset printing plates that causes non-image areas to accept water and repel ink.

Developer
A chemical solution that transforms a latent image on film or paper into a visible image.

Developing Tank
A container used for processing film.

Diaphragm
The adjustable opening behind a camera lens.

Die Cut
The mechanical process of cutting shapes in paper.

Direct Bundle or Sack
A sack or bundle of direct-mail pieces all going to one post office.

Direct Color Separation
A color separation made through a halftone screen.

Direct Mail
Advertisements made directly to the consumer through a mailing piece.

Display Advertisement
An advertisement in a periodical that usually contains illustrations and a variety of type sizes and styles.

Display Type
Type set larger than body copy.

Distribution
The marketing or merchandising of commodities.

Dodging
The blocking of light in certain areas when exposing paper in an enlarger

Dot Area, Dot Percentage
The percentage of the area in a halftone screen occupied by dots.

Double Exposure
Two pictures superimposed on one piece of film or paper, usually done accidentally, sometimes done intentionally for special effect.

Double Spread
Art or type that covers two facing pages.

Dry Mount
The process of adhering artwork to a board using heat applied to specially prepared paper between the two.

Dummy
A fairly accurate representation of a printed piece before actually preparing a finished paste-up.

Duotone
A method of producing exceptionally sharp halftones from the combination of two negatives.

Duplicator
An office machine used for printing reproductions of typed or drawn copy.

Dust Jacket or Wrapper
The paper folded over the cover of a book.

Earned Rate
The cost per column-inch or agate line achieved by an advertiser by virtue of having

purchased a large quantity of advertising space.

Elite
Typewriter type with 12 characters to the inch.

EM
1. The square size of any type body.
2. A pica.

Emulsion
The gelatin coating of light-sensitive material on photographic film or paper.

En
Half the width of an em.

Enamel
Glossy, coated paper.

Englargement
A print larger than the original negative.

Enlarger
A device used to project an image from a negative on photographic paper.

Exchange Advertisement
An advertisement placed in one periodical by the publisher of another who will extend the same privilege to that periodical which accepted his ad.

Expire
A subscriber to a periodical who has not renewed the subscription.

Exposure
The density and duration of light on photographic film, paper, or plate.

Exposure Meter
A device with light-sensitive cell that measures the amount of light in a given area.

Extended Type
A type face wider than it is usually printed.

Face
A style of type.

Family
All the varieties of one type face such as light, bold italic, condensed, and extended.

Fanzine
Originally a periodical written by and for science fiction enthusiasts, but often now referring to any special interest magazine.

Ferrotype Plate
A chromium-plated metal sheet used for drying photographs to achieve a glossy finish.

Film Speed
The sensitivity of a film to light.

Filter
A colored piece of glass placed over a lens to change,

in some way, the nature of the image in the resulting photo.

Fixed Focus Lens
A camera lens that is not adjustable for various distances.

Fixing Bath
A solution that causes sensitized film or paper to no longer react to light.

Flap
A piece of tissue placed over artwork for protection and for indicating changes and corrections.

Flat
1. A photograph low in contrast.
2. A camera-ready mounted paste-up.

Flattener
A solution used to dry prints that prevents their curling.

Flop
To turn a negative over so that it prints a mirror image.

Flush Left, Flush Right
Copy set with one edge, either left or right, straight and the other ragged.

Focus
The adjustment of a lens to sharply define an image.

Fold-out
A page in a book or periodical that unfolds to increase the size of the page.

Font
A film or matrix for producing usable type.

Form 3579
The Postal Service form used to comply with "Address Correction Requested."

Format
The general size, shape and style of a book or periodical.

Foundry Type
Metal type used for hand composition.

Fountain Solution
The water solution used on offset presses to coat the printing plate in non-image areas thereby preventing ink from adhering.

Four-color Process
The method by which printing is done to achieve a full-color effect.

Frequency Discount
A lower rate given to advertisers who repeat an ad unchanged.

Fulfillment
The responsibility of assuring that mail-order buyers receive what they have ordered.

Galley
1. A metal tray used to hold type.
2. Proof of type that has been set.

Gang-up
To print or photograph one or more articles at one time.

Gatefold
See Fold-out.

Gather
Assembling folded signatures in sequence.

Glossy
Shiny paper or photograph.

Gothic
Type faces without serifs.

Grain
1. The direction of the fibers in paper or cardboard.
2. The granular appearance of a negative or picture.

Graphic Arts
The general term to describe the occupation of one involved in the preparation of artwork, typography, and photography for reproduction.

Grid
The pre-determined page layout format for a magazine.

Grippers
The little fingers on a press that pull through a piece of paper.

Ground Glass
The sheet of glass in the back of a process camera on which an image is focused.

Gumming
The protection of the non-image areas of a printing plate with gum arabic.

Gutter
The inner margin of a book or periodical page.

Halftone
A photo or drawing that has been translated into dots of various sizes in order to give the appearance of gray tones.

Halftone Screen
See Contact Screen.

Headliner
An apparatus used to set larger sizes of type photographically.

House Organ
A periodical that circulates among the employees of a company.

Hypo
See Fixing Solution.

Image
The general term for anything (pictures, type, etc.) that is to be reproduced.

Image Area
That part of a negative or

plate that contains the image to be reproduced.

Impost
An extra charge to advertisers for premium placement of an ad, such as the back cover, inside front cover, etc.

Imprint
A publisher's name and date of publication printed in a book.

Inadmissable Enclosure
Anything included in a piece of mail that the Postal Service deems nonconformable within the rules for that particular class of mail.

In-house   Work done on the premises rather than being hired out.

Initial Letters
A large letter used at the beginning of a paragraph or chapter.

Ink Roller
On a printing press, those rollers that carry ink to or apply it on the plate.

Insert
Anything placed in a periodical that is not a standard page.

Intaglio
A printing process by which ink is transferred from wells etched into the plate on to the surface to be printed.

ISBN,ISSN
International Standard Book Number, International Standard Serial Number. An internationally accepted code for the identification of individual books and periodicals.

Italics
Type that slants to the right.

Justify
To set type so that all lines in a column are of equal length.

Kern
Part of a letter that extends beyond the body of the letter.

Layout
The arrangement of the various elements on the paste-up.

Layout Sheets
Sheets pre-printed with guide-lines in non-reproducible blue ink.

Leading

The extra spacing between lines of type.

Legibility

The speed with which an individual letter can be recognized.

Lens

The optical glass in a camera through which light is focused to form an image on film or paper.

Lens Speed

The largest opening at which the diaphragm behind a lens can be set.

Libel

A defamatory statement for which an aggrieved party can collect damages.

Lift-off Letters

Letters printed on adhesive back acetate that can be cut out and placed in position on artwork.

Ligature

Two or more letters combined to make a single character.

Light Table

A back-lighted piece of glass used as a work area that enables one to see through the material on the glass.

Line

Any artwork (type, drawing, tone-line photo or whatever) that can be photographed without using a halftone screen.

Line-for-line

Copy that is to be set in lines just the way it is typed.

Line Gauge

A printer's measuring rule.

Linotype

A machine for setting type in metal.

List Broker

An individual or firm selling mailing lists.

Lithography

The process by which material is printed from a flat surface (as opposed to letterpress or intalgio) where the image is ink receptive and blank areas are ink repellent.

Little Magazine

Non-commercial periodical.

Logo or **Logotype**

A trademark or name that has been designed to be used exclusively to represent a particular firm or individual.

Lower Case

The small letters of an alphabet.

Magenta

One of the three basic color inks used in full-color printing (red).

Magenta Screen

See Contact Screen

Mailing Permit

An agreement with the Postal Service to make bulk mailings at lower than first class rates after certain fees have been paid and certain conditions met.

Makeready

The preparation of a press just prior to printing.

Manuscript

Original writing that has not been set in type.

Margin

The white space on a sheet of paper between the image area and the edge of the sheet.

Mask

The covering of unwanted portions of negatives or artwork.

Masthead

A block of printed matter, usually in the upper left-hand corner of a page, giving the name of the periodical, its address, the date of publication, and the names of those associated with its publication.

Mat

A frame cut in cardboard to surround a piece of artwork.

Mat Knife

A knife with replaceable blades used for trimming cardboard.

Matte Finish

A surface that is without gloss.

Matrix (or Mat)

A metal or cardboard mold in which metal is cast for making a raised printing surface.

Mechanical

A camera-ready paste-up.

Microform

Microfilm or microfiche. Greatly reduced film positives or negatives of printed pages that can be projected on a screen for reading purposes.

Milline Rate

The cost per agate line for every thousand readers of an advertisement.

Mimeograph

An office duplicator for making copies of printed matter through the use of special stencils stretched over a roller and through which ink is pressed.

Moire

A usually unwanted pattern that develops from the improper rescreening of a halftone print.

Monochrome

Printed in a single color.

Morgue

A periodical's collection of references, news clippings, and photos.

Ms.

Manuscript.

Multiwell

The grouping of a periodical's editorial matter in clusters.

Negative

Developed film that has a reverse-tone image.

Nixie

A mailing piece returned to a mailer in response to "Address Correction Requested."

Nth Name Selection

A fractional unit repeated in sampling a mailing list (as every 10th name, or every 7th name).

OCR

See Optical Character Recognition.

Offprint

A magazine article reprinted in quantity to be sold or given away.

Offset Lithography

The lithographic process whereby the image is transferred to a second surface and from there printed on the paper.

Offsetting

The accidental transference of wet ink from one printed sheet of paper to another.

Opacity

The quality of printing paper that prevents any printing from showing through from the reverse side or from another sheet.

Opaqueing

The painting over of unwanted material on a negative from which a printing plate is to be made.

Optical Character Recognition

The process by which computers can "read" typewritten copy and automatically set type.

Orthochromatic

Film sensitive to most colors but red.

Outline Halftone

A halftone picture from which the background has been eliminated.

Outsert

Something attached to the cover of a periodical.

Overexposure

The condition where too much light reaches a sensitized surface.

Overlay

Any sheet on top artwork. See Acetate Overlay and Tissue Overlay.

Overrun

The printing of more pieces than were ordered.

Padding Compound

The adhesive used in binding pads of paper along one edge.

Pagination

The planning or numbering of pages in their proper sequential order.

Paid Circulation

Subscriptions to a magazine that have actually been paid for.

Pamphlet

A small booklet, usually with a soft cover.

Panchromatic

Film that is sensitive to various tones of color at approximately the same level as the human eye.

Paperbound

A book or magazine with a flexible cover.

Paste-up

The assembling and adhesion of various elements in their proper places in preparation for photography.

Perfect Binding

A method of binding whereby the paper is trimmed and then glued together rather than sewed.

Photocomposition

The photographic setting of type on sensitized paper.

Photoengraving

A relief engraving on metal using photographic methods.

Photolithography

See Offset Lithography.

Pica

A printer's measure equal to 1/6 of an inch.

Pica Pole

Jocular name for Line Gauge.

Pica Typewriter

A typewriter that prints 10 characters to the inch.

Planographic

A method of printing such as lithography that transfers ink from a flat surface.

Plate

The printing surface that carries the image to be transferred.

PMT

Photomechanical Transfer. Eastman Kodak's method of making photographic prints for further reproduction.

Point

1. A printer's measure equal to 1/72 of an inch.

2. A unit to measure the thickness of paper and stock equivalent to 1/1000 of an inch.

Polychrome

Printing in three or more colors.

Positive

An image with the same tonal values as the original subject.

Posterization

A method by which a continuous tone photo is reduced to only a few tones.

Pound

Paper weight (20-pound, 60-pound) determined by the weight of one ream (500 sheets) of paper cut to a standard size.

Print

A positive picture usually printed on paper or Mylar.

Process Camera

The large stationary camera used by printers to photograph halftones, prints, and offset negatives.

Progressive Proofs

A set of proofs showing the individual colors of a multicolored printing.

Proof

A duplication from plates, negatives or paste-ups before printing showing how the final printed product will look.

Proofread

To read proofs for correctness before printing.

Proportional Wheel

A device for determining the enlargement or reduction of artwork in order to maintain the same proportions as the original.

Psychographics

Characteristics and qualities of the lifestyles and attitudes of a particular mailing list.

Public Domain

The realm embracing writings and artwork that may be reproduced by anyone.

Purge

The process of eliminating duplicates or unwanted names from a mailing list.

Quarterly

1. Any periodical published four times a year.

2. A name often applied to literary journals usually published every three months.

Quire

1. A set of folded sheets in a booklet fitting one within another.

2. 24 sheets, usually applied now to mimeograph stencils.

Quote

The predetermined charges of a printer for completing a job.

Rag Content Paper

A better grade of paper made wholly or partly from rags.

Ragged Right, Ragged Left

Type set in a column with either the left or right edge left unjustified.

Readership

The number of actual readers of a periodical as opposed to the circulation.

Ream

500 sheets of paper cut to size.

Recto

A right-hand page.

Reflex Camera

A camera where the image to be photographed is reflected on a screen where it may be viewed. In a single lens reflex, the scene is viewed through the same lens that takes the picture. In a twin lens reflex the scene is viewed through a separate lens.

Remainders

A publisher's overstocked titles that are no longer selling well, usually offered at a reduced price.

Renewal Notice

A reminder to a subscriber that a subscription to a periodical has expired, usually with an exhortation to renew.

Reprint

One or more copies of a portion of a book or periodical

reproduced by other than the original publisher.

Reproducible
A piece of artwork or a print capable of maintaining a reasonable degree of quality when reproduced.

Reproduction Proof
A proof taken from metal type of sharp enough quality to be photographically reproduced.

Repros
See Reproduction Proof.

Resized Typography
Type that is photographed larger or smaller than the original.

Reticulation
A crackling of film emulsion during processing for special effect (or by a processing error).

Retouching
Altering a print or negative after developing to change its appearance.

Return Privilege
The right of a book dealer to return unsold copies for full refund.

Reverse
A print in which what was white on the original becomes black and vice versa.

Review Copy
A copy of a book or periodical sent free to a periodical for the purpose of its being publicly evaluated.

Review Journal
A periodical that specializes in reviewing other published works.

Right Reading
An image on film or paper that reads correctly from left to right.

Roman
A type style with thick and thin strokes in the letters and having serifs.

ROP
Run of Press.

Rough
A preliminary sketch of a layout.

Royalty
The money paid to an author as his share of the revenue from the sale of his work.

Rule
A usually straight, unadorned printed line.

Rule Box
A frame composed of rules.

Run of Press
An advertisement or use of color to be placed anywhere in

a periodical at the discretion of the publisher.

Saddle Stitching
A method of binding where staples are placed through the folded edge of a book or periodical.

Safelight
A darkroom light giving forth illumination to which film or paper being exposed is not sensitive.

Same Size
Instructions to a cameraman to reproduce a piece of artwork neither larger nor smaller than the original.

Sample Mailing
The sending of a direct-mail advertisement to just a portion of a mailing list as a test of the list's value in providing responses.

Sans Serif
A typeface without serifs.

Scale
Maintaining the original proportions of a piece of artwork during enlargement or reduction.

SCF
A U.S. Postal Service regional distribution center comprising many different post offices whose ZIP codes all start with the same first three numbers.

Scoring
The creasing of a piece of paper or heavy stock to facilitate folding.

Screen
A piece of film or plastic with a regular pattern of dots or other marks and used to transfer that pattern to another surface.

Screened Paper Print
A photographic halftone made on paper to be photographed as line copy (copy dot).

Screen Tint
The effect obtained when placing a screen over a clear section of a negative to achieve that pattern on a plate or print.

Script
Manuscript.

Seed Money
The first stage financing of a proposed magazine before

coming to the decision to actually make a major investment.

Separation
One of the plates used in printing a job of more than one color.

Serial Rights
The negotiated right of a periodical to publish and republish or limit further publication of a manuscript, piece of art, or photograph.

Serif
A short line stemming from the end of a letter.

Sharpness
Clean edges, fully in focus.

Shoot
To photograph.

Sig Cut
See Logotype.

Signature
1. The section of a book or periodical obtained from the folding of a larger sheet of paper on which 16 or 32 pages are printed.
2. See Logotype.

Silverprint
A photographic proof provided by a printer.

Single Copy Sales
Newsstand sales of a periodical.

Single Lens Reflex
See Reflex Camera.

Slug
Either a line of metal type or a piece of metal used as spacing between lines of type.

SLR
See Reflex Camera.

Small Caps
Capital letters the same size as lower case letters in a line of type.

Small Press
A non-commercial publisher.

Softbound
See Paperbound.

Soft Focus
A photograph resulting from a special lens that, although generally in focus, has soft rather than sharp outlines.

Solarization
A reversal in gradation sequence of a photograph achieved by exposing the print to additional light during development.

Solid
1. An image area printed with no screen tone.
2. Type set with no extra leading.

Specs
Specifications for type, printing, paper, or binding.
Spine
The bound edge of a book or periodical.
Split Fountain
The separating of ink in the press to achieve multi-color printing with just one pass through the press.
Split Test
Two or more samples of the same mailing list, each considered to be representative, to test different approaches or to test the homogeneity of the list.
Square Serif
A type face with uniformly thick serifs.
Stamping
The printing done with ink or foil on the cover of a clothbound book.
Stop Bath
The intermediate step between developing solution and fixing bath in the development of pictures or negatives.
Subhead
A small headline within the text.
Subscription Agency
A company that takes the responsibility for ordering subscriptions to periodicals for a third party.
Subsidiary Rights
The sale of written work for other than what it was originally contracted: movies, serialization in magazines, book clubs, paperback publication, etc.
Tabloid
A newspaper size usually 11" x 17"
Tearsheet
A page torn from a periodical usually presented to an advertiser as verification of an ad's publication.
Template
A pattern or guide for drawing specific shapes.
Text
1. See Body Copy.
2. A typeface resembling Old English.
TF
See Till Forbid.
Thick and Thin
Any typeface that has a variety of line thicknesses in its letters.
Think Money
See Advance.

Thumbnail Sketch
The initial rough sketch of a proposed layout, usually done much smaller than the finished layout.
Till Forbidden
Used by advertisers and subscribers to indicate that an advertisement should be repeated on a regular basis or that a subscription should be continually renewed until orders are given otherwise.
Tint
A pastel shade or gray tone achieved by printing with a screen rather than as a solid color.
Tip-in
An individual sheet of paper pasted into a book.
Tipping Compound
The adhesive used for tip-ins.
Tissue Overlay
A piece of tissue paper laid over artwork both for protection and for showing changes and corrections.
TLR
See Reflex Camera.
Tone-line
The process making line illustrations from continuous tone photos.
Transfer Lettering
Letters that can be pressed and burnished onto a surface from a translucent sheet of plastic or paper.
Trial Subscriber
A subscriber to a periodical for a short period at, usually, a reduced price.
Trim Size
The actual finished dimensions of a printed work.
Type Gauge
See Line Gauge.
Type High
0.918 inch. This is the standard height in letterpress printing from the impression surface of type to its base.
Typo or Typographical Error
A misspelled word or other mistake in typesetting.
Twins Lens Reflex
See Reflex Camera.
Two-up, Three-up, etc.
Printing more than one copy of a given image at the same time on a single sheet of paper.
Underexposure
A condition where too little light has reached photographic paper, negative, or printing plate.

Underrun
The printing of fewer than were ordered.
Unjustified
Type that is usually set flush left but ragged right.
Uppercase
Capital letters.
Vanity Press
A general term for publishers who will print whatever authors pay them to print with no consideration of literary or social merit.
Variable Contrast Paper
Photographic paper that provides different degrees of contrast when exposed through special filters.
Verso
A left-hand page in a book or periodical.
Vignette
A portion of a photo achieved by shading the remainder from exposure.
Waxer
A devise used for applying a wax adhesive to the back of type or artwork before application to a layout.
Web Press
A printing press that prints on paper from rolls rather than single sheets.
Whole Number
The actual sequential number of a periodical.
White-out
The painting out with an opaque white solution of an unwanted element on a layout.
White Space
The area in a layout not covered by type or illustrations.
Widow
A word or two at the top of a page ending a paragraph from the preceding page.
Window
A piece of material that will leave a clear space on a negative for the stripping-in of another negative.
Wrapper
See Dust Jacket.
Wrong Font
A letter of one typeface inserted into a line of another typeface.
Yellow
One of the three basic color inks used in full-color printing.
ZIP Code Sequence
The arrangement of mailing pieces in numerical order by ZIP code.

Index